NATURE STUDY COLLECTIVE

174 Lessons for Nature Field Trips

JAMIE CURRENT

To my favorite hiking buddies
Olivia, Calvin, and Korban.
May you know God's Word
and God's World.

And to my husband Brandon,
With you I would go anywhere.

ISBN: 978-0-578-93725-0

www.naturestudycollective.com

NATURE STUDY COLLECTIVE

174 Lessons for Nature Field Trips

JAMIE CURRENT

"We were all meant to be naturalists, each in his degree, and it is inexcusable to live in a world so full of the marvels of plant and animal life and to care for none of these things."

Charlotte Mason,
"Home Education"

Contents

Nature Study Lessons

"We all have need to be trained to see, and to have our eyes opened before we can take in the joy that is meant for us in this beautiful life. An observant child should be put in the way of things worth observing."

Charlotte Mason
"Home Education"

About
Nature
Study

About Nature Study

We live in a spectacularly interesting world. There are countless natural wonders just outside our door: birds are caring for babies and fetching dinner, insect societies are rising or falling, and shoots and roots are breaking forth from tiny seeds. The natural world operates without human involvement and, too often, its notice.

As educators, we have the opportunity and joy of putting our students in touch with this fascinating realm. By studying nature, they become at home in their world and familiar with its non-human inhabitants. The Nature Study approach preserves the thrill of discovery and the wonder of creation.

However, as simple as this sounds it can be intimidating! Many of us were educated with dry textbooks inside classroom walls. We remember well the drudgery of long worksheets. Yet, we may not know wildlife beyond dandelions and houseflies. There is a good chance we will not have answers to the questions our kids will raise when we take them outside.

The Nature Study approach, thankfully, does not require an all-knowing teacher. It is normal to say, "I don't know. Let's find out together!" In fact, the job is not to give the students information but to provide the opportunity for *them* to find out all they can. Specifically, the educator needs to reserve time for outdoor exploration and provide resources (like field guides) for their students. Encouragement and structure are all that is needed.

The educator must only be eager to learn alongside the students and willing to facilitate the process. This book was written to inspire and equip those who want to make that happen. The following pages explain what nature study is, give practical instructions in how to do it, and provide specific lessons to accomplish with your students.

Nature Study in Education

Nature Study became an educational movement in the 19th and 20th centuries. It was promoted by scientists and educators with the goal of teaching students about the natural world while encouraging them to care about it. The slogan "study nature, not books" summarized its primary idea: we learn more effectively through firsthand experience than secondhand instruction.

Thankfully, these ideas did not stay in the past. Some public schools, private schools, and homeschools have put nature study into practice by immersing their students in nature and encouraging them to use their five senses to gain knowledge. In addition, educators across many teaching philosophies utilize hands-on outdoor excursions in nature to engage their students.

What is Nature Study?

At its core, nature study is learning about the natural world through the five senses.

Nature study is a **direct personal experience**. The children feel the flower's ridged petal, see the birds soaring above, smell the ocean breeze, taste the freshly picked garden vegetable, and hear the insects chirping. While reading about a subject is beneficial, experiencing it makes the knowledge real and lasting and theirs. Today's technology gives easy access to scientists, well-written books, and high-quality videos, yet nothing replaces real-life encounters to build interest and understanding.

Nature study utilizes **observation.** Students use their five senses-fueled by curiosity- to notice and learn. Educators should prompt and guide, but the children should be discovering the information for themselves. This exercise builds the skills of careful attention, thorough examination, and self-direction. These abilities are foundational to scientific study at all levels.

Nature study is about **connection**. Given the time and space to do so, we instinctively relate new information to what we already know. While observing a specimen, students may categorize, compare similarities, contrast differences, or remember something previously studied. With each nature study experience, students build an understanding of how nature works. In contrast, the analyzing process is overrun when the students are fed information and are required to parrot it back. Learning often becomes shallow and students become disengaged.

Nature study results in **recording.** The children sort through what they observed about the subject, connect it to what they already know, and communicate it on the pages of their blank nature journals. As they convey the information with their own words and drawings, learning solidifies into deeper understanding.

Nature Study Lessons

Educators typically focus on one or two nature topics per term, such as birds, or wildflowers and trees. They read aloud a book on the topic to lay foundational concepts. Each week, students are taken outdoors to **experience** the subject firsthand. It may be in the form of an object lesson or an encounter with it in its natural habitat. They learn all they can about the specimen by **observing** it with their senses. The teacher may ask prompting questions to help them notice more and **connect** it to their existing knowledge. The students then **record** what they learned in their nature journals using written notes, drawings, diagrams, and counts/measurements.

Not Only Nature Study

Though a significant part, nature study should not be the sole source of science education. Charlotte Mason had nature study as a core practice in her schools but advised, "The study of science should be pursued in an ordered sequence, which is not possible or desirable in a walk." (School Education, 237). A science curriculum should also be in place to cover necessary concepts systematically, including those beyond personal observation and the local environment. Many curriculums have a comprehensive plan that uses books, videos, experiments, and object lessons to accomplish this.

Why Nature Study?

Scientific Knowledge

Through nature study, students come to know about the world around them. This knowledge is firsthand, staying with them much like their other life experiences. Over time, they will recognize the local birds, trees, wildflowers, and insects. They will know their names, habits, where they live- just like old friends. They will understand how the world works as they observe the life cycle of plants growing from tiny seeds, see how animals live in their environments, and encounter evidence of the forces of nature shaping the seemingly stable face of the Earth. An essential foundation for the upper-level sciences forms in the process.

Love of Learning

Children who love to learn have an inward curiosity that motivates them. They are interested and engaged. All parents and teachers wish this for the kids in their care.

Thankfully, the love of learning is innate. Babies are born to learn without being taught how to do so. Toddlers ask innumerable questions every day, eager to know about the world around them. Unfortunately, things can change once school starts. Their job flips— instead of asking questions, they are now required to supply answers using memorized information. The goal becomes to finish the worksheet or pass the test or gain approval from the teacher. The simple joy of knowing can quickly be lost.

Science, however, is a curiosity-driven field. While students must learn an existing body of knowledge, all advances are attained by inquiring minds that investigate and try new things. The nature study approach fosters this discovery mentality. Children seek information to fulfill their curiosity, using their senses to learn. The method is outdoor exploration, the subject matter is tangible, and the test is a blank page for them to fill as they determine.

This method of learning is so instinctive to children that it bypasses their differing academic abilities. The children who struggle to focus during the hours of classroom seatwork become actively engaged learners when they are out in the fresh air. Those who have to work harder to understand information given through words and numbers are unhindered when handling physical objects. We level the field when we take science from abstract ideas to concrete participation. Learning is easier and more enjoyable for all.

Skills of Observation and Attention

Nature study exercises two habits that are key to all learning, regardless of subject: observation and attention. As children figure out the differences between two beetles or describe how ducks move across the pond, they develop the ability to get knowledge using their senses. They are observing with their focused attention as they perceive, categorize, distinguish, and collect information. Nature study, done regularly and intentionally, builds and strengthens these skills.

Observation and attention are necessary for all educational endeavors. This carefulness is used when learning about a topic through reading, understanding math problems, deciphering musical notation, following sound logic, and developing fine art abilities. During nature study, their efforts are rewarded and encouraged as they discover new and exciting concepts.

Communicating Information Well

Through nature study, children learn how to communicate information gained through their observations. As they encounter and study nature, they must mentally sort through their findings to choose how to record them in a nature journal. The pages are blank. Students fill them with drawings, written notes, diagrams, and measurements, as they determine. This process ensures that they truly understand the subject and gives them practice ordering their thoughts as they consider transmitting the information to others.

Appreciation

Becoming familiar with the natural world causes people to appreciate and care for it. Delving deep into the ingenious cycles designed in nature makes us all the more thankful for the fascinating world provided for us. It causes us to take care of it as well. No one studying beavers then litters up their habitat. Instead, we are motivated to preserve and protect it. Children educated with nature study make a deep connection to the natural world- a connection that may last their lifetime.

Challenge

Hiking through nature challenges kids in a different way than academics or athletics. The terrain can be rough, requiring careful navigation with both their minds and their bodies as they balance on a fallen log, jump from rock to rock, and choose each step up a sand dune. Children overcome fears when they touch a slimy worm and endure the discomfort of unfavorable weather.

Long hikes require endurance. It does not matter how tired the students get; they have to keep walking until they make it back to the parking lot. These opportunities for accomplishment help children gain self-control, confidence, and physical discipline.

Enjoyment

Finally, being at home in nature is delightful. Nature study has built-in exercise, fresh air, and time away from screens and the cares of everyday life. It is a refreshing change of pace. There are benefits to mental health, physical fitness, and overall well-being. Even when children and adults do not feel like going outside, they are glad they made the effort once there.

Through nature study, children may develop worthwhile pursuits that last for the rest of their lives. Gardening, bird watching, fishing, drawing, rock collecting, keeping pets, and hiking are hobbies that can extend into adulthood.

" All we find out may be old knowledge, and is most likely already recorded in books; but, for us, it is new, our own discovery, our personal knowledge, a little bit of the world's real work which we have attempted and done. However little work we do in this kind, we gain by it some of the power to appreciate, not merely beauty, but fitness, adaptation, processes. Reverence and awe grow upon us, and we are brought into a truer relation with the Almighty Worker."

Charlotte Mason
"Ourselves"

How To Do
Nature Study

How To Do Nature Study

Nature study is a firsthand experience in which students observe all they can about nature using their five senses, connect this new information to what they already know, and then record it in a nature journal. This chapter covers each part of that process in practical detail.

Make a Plan

To make nature study happen, you may find the "Nature Study Plan" on the next page helpful. A printable version is available on naturestudycollective.com. Schedule your outings for a regular time each week, such as every Friday afternoon or during the science time slot in your schedule.

The table of contents of this book has the major nature topics listed in alphabetical order. Choose one or two to focus on for the semester. Flip to that chapter and assign one lesson per outing. Some may take multiple weeks. These activities give your students the opportunity to experience, enjoy, and connect to the natural world themselves. Background information is provided where needed and each topic has an introduction to read along with suggested field guides to reference during your study.

Consider the season for which you are planning. In regions with frozen winters, fish may be difficult to encounter. However, studying the night sky is ideal since darkness falls before bedtime. Other topics, like trees, can be studied in all seasons.

Many topics have a lesson called "Study 12". If this is your first experience with nature study, do that activity each week for your first semester. It is easy to implement and gives a useful foundation to build on with future study.

Next, select nature locations near you that work with your lessons. Look for state parks, nature centers, forests, wildlife preserves, scenic parks, hiking trails, and local waterways. You do not need a new location every week. It is beneficial to do repeated visits to the same places, as children will discover new things and see changes over the seasons.

Finally, choose a read-aloud book about the nature topic to accompany your outings. It will give your children the framework and vocabulary to support their study. From a book, they learn how trees grow, spread, and produce fruit, while on their nature outings, they see and touch these truths in real life. Combining firsthand observation with the information from authors who are experts in their fields will give a well-rounded education. Begin each outing by reading a few pages from the nature book. The lesson and the readings do not have to coordinate.

This book provides a few recommendations for each topic. Pre-read them to ensure they are appropriate for your kids in terms of length, depth of information, and worldview. If your primary curriculum assigns books, use those. When finding your own selections, look for picture books that communicate an overview of the topic and include photographs, illustrations, and diagrams. The best options are written in literary form with beautiful, well-crafted language. Avoid books that are disjointed collections of facts.

Once settled, fill in the read-aloud(s), dates, locations, activities, page numbers, and special supplies needed on your plan. This sheet will serve as a helpful reference before you go out each week. Obtain the field guides, supplies, and read-alouds prior to starting nature study.

Nature Study Plan

Available as a printable on naturestudycollective.com.

Subject: _____

Read-Aloud Book(s): _____

Outings

Done	Date	Lesson Title	Lesson Page Number	Special Supplies Needed	Location

Gather Your Supplies

Before your first outing, prepare the things you will need. Some families put everything into one backpack that is carried by the parent. Other families, groups, or classes have each child carry their supplies in their own bag.

Each child will need the following:

- **Nature journal**
  Choose a blank, spiral-bound sketchbook with a hard cover. This is ideal for using outside, but any blank notebook will do. If you are painting, choose one with heavy paper to prevent bleed-through.

- **Drawing/painting supplies**
  Use a simple pencil, a set of colored pencils, or a palate of watercolor paints.

- **Field guide or identification app**
  Use reference books or apps to learn about what you find. Bring them along or leave them in the vehicle to consult after the hike. They may be shared by multiple students.

- **Appropriate clothing**
  Rain boots or waterproof hiking shoes and clothes that can get dirty allow kids to explore wherever interest leads. Outfits suited for the weather make hiking more comfortable.

- **Special supplies needed for your activity**
  Some of the lessons in this book require special supplies, such as tape, a shovel, or a fishing pole. Read through the lesson and note it on your nature study plan.

Optional:

- **Lidded jar with poked holes and a plastic storage bag**
  Lightweight containers are handy when bringing back a nature find, such as a caterpillar or a messy seed pod.

- **Magnifying glass, travel microscope, binoculars**
  These instruments help kids see more while exploring.

- **Bug spray**
  Insect repellent is necessary for some seasons and in some locations.

- **Water and snacks**
  For some kids, having something to munch on helps them stay out longer. You could stop at a halfway spot to work in nature journals, have your snack, and play before heading back to the parking lot.

Set Up Your Nature Journal

Children should write their names and grades on the inside of the front cover. If the journal is misplaced, including a phone number would enable someone to return it to you.

Inside the back cover, create a ruler to use for measuring while outside. Line up a ruler vertically along the cover edge and mark every inch or centimeter, whichever units you prefer, from the bottom all the way up to the top.

Students can copy down these lists on the first page of their journals to reference if they get stuck while doing an entry:

Observe By:

Looking
Feeling
Hearing
Smelling
Tasting (if safe)

Ways to Show Information:

Main Drawing
Alternate-view Drawing
Diagram
Written Notes
Measurements
Counts and Estimates

Go Outside!

Now you are ready for your first nature study outing. Remember, the process of nature study is experiencing, observing, connecting, and recording.

Experiencing

Start by reading aloud a few pages of your selected read-aloud book.

Next, either explain the scheduled activity to your kids or read it to them, reserving the provided questions for later use. If background information is given, read it to them or use it for your own knowledge as you guide the activity.

Before hiking, lay some guiding rules, such as:

1. Stay behind a leading adult.

2. Anyone can stop the group if they notice something interesting along the way, even if it is not related to the lesson.

3. We will do our hiking, lesson, and nature journaling first, then have free time.

Then, head out to accomplish the lesson. Do not rush through the steps. Give students time to experience nature rather than merely finish the assignment.

Observing

Every lesson has the children observing nature. As they do so, remind them to use their senses to learn everything they can about the subject. They should touch, smell, look at, listen to, and, in a few cases, even taste the nature item they are studying.

Give them time to notice. Educators should gently direct but not feed students the information. Most lessons include questions the teacher can ask to aid student discovery.

Connecting

This step flows seamlessly from observation, but it is worth noting. The children use their existing knowledge to understand these new things. They may compare how a nature item is the same or different from another they had learned about previously. They may group their nature finds in categories. The tangible specimen may remind them of what they learned from the read-aloud. This connecting step is encouraged by the prompting questions given in the lesson.

Recording

Each lesson directs the children to open their nature journals and record their learning. See the next few pages for examples.

Keep everything organized by giving each entry its own page. Include a prominent title with the name of the specimen studied, using a field guide or nature app to identify it. This book has field guide recommendations given in the introduction to each topic. Write the location of where you found the item and the date.

The body of the entry should include as much information as possible about the nature subject. The children choose how to communicate what they learned. They draw or paint a picture to show what it looks like. They might pair the main drawing with another from an alternate angle. For example, they could depict a butterfly with its wings flat in the main sketch and add an alternate illustration with its wings resting vertically. Sometimes a diagram is most clear, such as the flight pattern of a bird or the flow of a stream. Details that are hard to illustrate should be explained in writing. Words can convey textures or express how an animal crawls, for example. For quantities that can be measured, counted, or estimated, these are shown in numbers. The most thorough journal entries will incorporate many of these elements.

If a child is struggling with their nature journal entry, ask them how they would describe it to someone who has never seen it before. Also, refer them to the "Observe By" and "Ways to Show Information" lists copied in their journals. These helpful lists are described on the previous page of this book. Nature journaling is a skill that is developed with practice; be prepared to give your students time and encouragement. Initial entries may be simple and wanting. Kids will certainly learn more than they put on the page.

Remember, also, the goal is not to create beautiful nature art but to capture information. Artistic children will undoubtedly enjoy making graceful drawings, but they must be accurate and thorough. Non-artistic children should not be discouraged by their abilities if they have filled their page with their observations, however un-framable they may feel their illustrations are.

These pages become a personal treasure that holds memories of good days and serves as a reference when you encounter your subject in nature again.

Sample Nature Journal Entries

Olivia, age 9

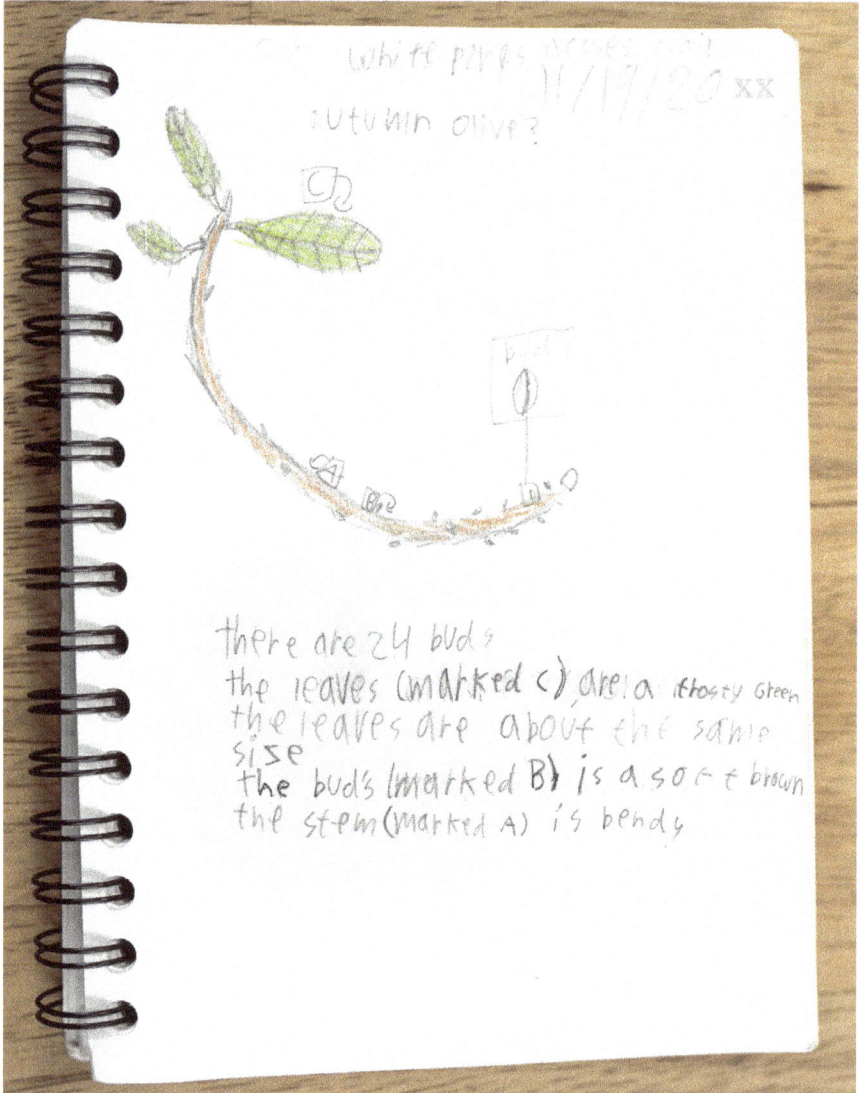

Calvin, age 6, scribed by a parent

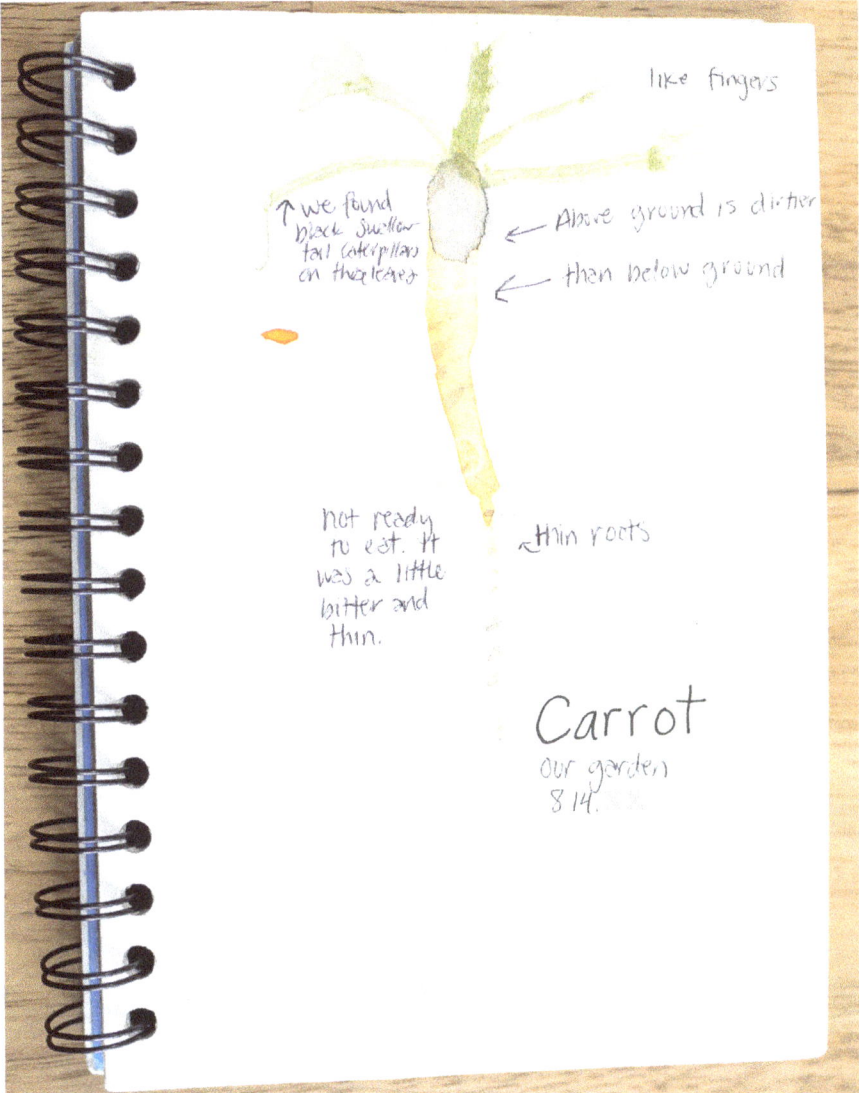

like fingers

we found black swallowtail caterpillars on the leaves

Above ground is dirtier

then below ground

not ready to eat. It was a little bitter and thin.

thin roots

Carrot
our garden
8 14.

Korban, age 4, scribed by a parent

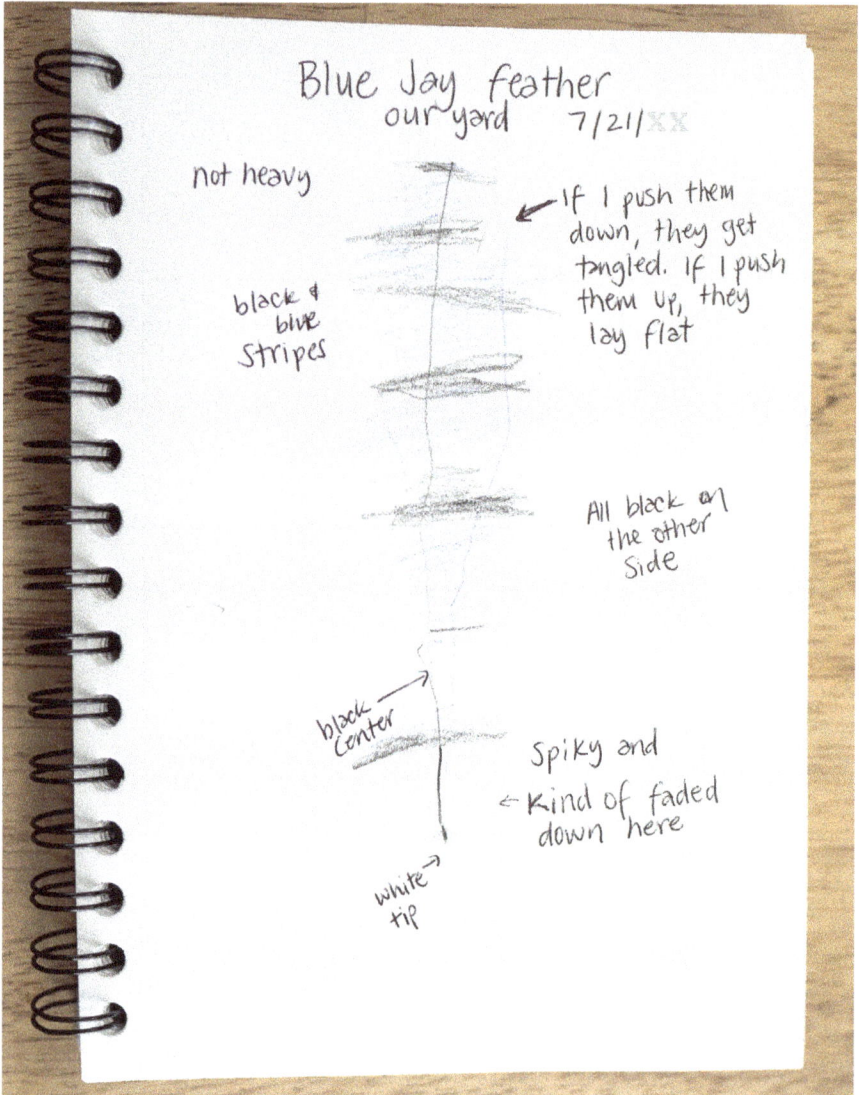

Tips

Hiking

If your children are unaccustomed to hiking, start with short trails or plan on turning around partway. They will build up endurance and interest with experience.

Hiking in the winter is more enjoyable when everyone is properly equipped. Wear wool socks and waterproof boots and gloves. Insert heat packs as a fun treat on very chilly days.

Protect yourself against ticks. These tiny creatures wait on the tips of tall grasses to jump onto passing mammals, including humans. They bury their heads into the skin to feed for several hours. A small percentage of them carry disease, though they have to be attached for an extended period of time for it to transmit. To prevent tick bites, walk in the center of established nature trails. Wear long sleeves and pants of lighter-colored fabrics, as it makes ticks easier to spot. Clothes can be treated with permethrin as a repellant. Check for ticks when you return to your vehicle. As an extra precaution, do a thorough body check back at home, shower, and wash and dry your clothes.

Observing

To help your kids notice more about a nature object, ask them how they would describe it to someone who is blind. This inspires close examination and a clear explanation.

Binoculars are helpful when looking at nature from a distance, but they can be tricky for young kids to master. Tell the child to look at the subject while you raise the binoculars to their eyes.

Journaling

Make the expectations for nature journaling clear to your students. Instruct them to fill at least one page, or require them work for a set amount of time. Fifteen minutes is a good target for elementary-aged beginners. Like all educational assignments, the goal is to challenge without overwhelming them. Another possibility is to leave journaling entirely optional. In traditional nature study, entries are not graded nor corrected for spelling or handwriting. These evaluations can discourage interest and distract from the main goals.

For kids who need a rigid structure, try dividing their nature journal page into boxes. They can fill each frame with a drawing, an alternate view, a diagram, written notes, or measurements as they choose.

For kids who are not yet writing fluently, you could "scribe" for them, copying what they say onto the page beside their illustrations.

To encourage more thorough and accurate work, try having everyone share their page with the group when finished. This structure has the added benefits of learning from each other and giving opportunity for public speaking.

Lead by example; keep your own nature journal alongside your kids. They will be interested in what you observed and how you chose to communicate it. At the same time, they will see scientific learning and recording modeled.

Just Start

Some people, after reading these pages, are excited and ready to head outdoors for nature study. Others want to do it all but are overwhelmed. My advice is to just start.

A Simple Outing

1. Commit to a time and choose a place.

2. Observe one thing well. Ask your kids to tell you about it, noticing as much as they can. Make it a competition if that helps. Remind them to use their five senses.

3. Then, open up your nature journals to record at least one interesting thing.

Going Deeper

Over time, being out in nature will become a habit. Children develop interest and observation skills, looking longer and more insightfully. They more effectively communicate what they learned in their journal. Be patient with the process as these abilities form.

Add in more elements to expand your nature study as you feel ready for them. Focus on a specific nature topic for the term/semester. Choose a book to read aloud and schedule a few lessons. Increase how often you head out. Extend the amount of time you work in your journals. As you and your students become more confident in nature study, work toward implementing the full structure.

"Failure"

Even with the best planning and effort, some nature outings are frustrating. Kids complain and are resistant. The subject you were hoping to encounter eludes you. The weather makes being outdoors miserable. While those days happen, being in nature is always profitable with new experiences- pleasant or otherwise. Tired kids may complain that they cannot possibly take another step, but they will make it back to the car. Next time, they will remember the accomplishment. Difficult circumstances are opportunities for growing more resilient.

As a teacher, you may feel embarrassed by your lack of knowledge. You may not be able to tell if a nature find is an insect, seed, or animal dropping. However, the greater lesson is demonstrating an eagerness to find out. Learn alongside your kids. Live out humility. We all start out not knowing, and it is only through interest and experience that we gain understanding. It is a privilege to develop this with our kids.

Remember that the teacher's job is not to give the answers but to encourage students to discover, observe, and connect with nature themselves. You will not have all the answers and you will not do everything right. No one does. However, you can model, facilitate and encourage a love of learning about nature. That is exactly what your students need.

For Families

Homeschool families can use this book to build their nature science lessons by following the planning steps on the preceding pages. Non-homeschool families can do these activities as they intentionally raise their children to be lifelong learners outside of the classroom.

The lessons work well for a wide range of ages. Older children observe nature more thoroughly, while younger kids collect an overall understanding of the topic. At every level, children are discovering knowledge for themselves and learning to communicate it.

Families with very young children can adapt nature study to meet their needs. You can write for children who are not able to do it comfortably on their own or keep a family nature journal and work together to make the entries. While hiking, consider letting the slowest walker/youngest family member lead the group. Older siblings will have more time to look around at the unhurried pace.

Doing nature study as a family is more flexible than in classes or groups. When sickness, scheduling conflicts, or inclement weather disrupt the plan, it is easily reworked. Also, families can do nature study outside of the daytime classroom hours. Kids can see the starry sky after dinner or explore natural rock formations while on vacation.

Nature study becomes part of your family culture rather than a school subject. Exploring together, learning new things, and enjoying the natural world makes for a rich childhood.

For Classroom Teachers

Classroom teachers can use these ideas for inquiry-based outdoor field trips, supplementing the curriculum they are teaching indoors. While covering butterflies, the class can be taken out to find caterpillars on the plants they naturally feed on and watch them day by day as they transform. This is so much more engaging and impactful than looking at pictures in a textbook.

As you plan your lessons, consider the subjects covered in your natural science curriculum. Incorporate the activities from this book that are feasible for your situation. If your school has a patch of trees within walking distance, nature study can be done. Many of the lessons are free and appropriate for a variety of ages.

The students can keep a nature journal of their experiences over the school year, share their entries in small groups or in front of the class for "show and tell," and take them home to continue on their own at summer break.

Nature study efforts lift science concepts out of the pages of their books and bring them into the real world. Students have tangible experiences and learn to use their senses to gain knowledge for themselves.

For Group Leaders

Use this book for structuring nature walks for a homeschool co-op or local nature hiking group. When students have a definite aim, as the lessons describe in this book, learning is focused and intentional. Everyone gets more out of the time.

Most activities in this book can be done with big groups or small ones and are appropriate for a wide range of ages. Groups can be open; families drop in and out as their schedule allows, or closed; families are expected to attend every meeting. An open group is a great way to introduce nature study to families unfamiliar with it. A closed group builds tighter-knit relationships.

Before you start, make sure all families are on the same page about nature study. The primary idea is that parents provide the time and opportunity outside, but it is the students who must discover for themselves. Parents who know about the subject may give a few words of direction or answer questions raised by the kids, but they should be careful that it does not turn into a lecture. Kids will quickly lose interest and stop observing for themselves.

HOW TO DO NATURE STUDY

Nature study in groups has many benefits. Parents and students enjoy hiking together, connecting on a social level while experiencing new things. On days when parents might stay indoors and skip nature study, an organized group ensures it happens. While outdoors, children spur each other on in learning and exploring. Timid children are emboldened by the more adventurous. A group might allow each child time for public speaking as they "show and tell" about a nature find collected between meetings. Parents who feel uncomfortable with natural science can utilize the enthusiasm and resources of other parents in the group to give their children these beneficial experiences.

Additional Resources

The *Handbook of Nature Study* by Anna Botsford Comstock is the classic resource for teaching the parent/educator about a wide range of nature topics. The book is organized with in-depth lessons for studying specific plants, animals, and other nature subjects based in the United States. The author was instrumental in promoting the nature study movement in its early days.

John Muir Laws is a present-day naturalist who produces books and videos about nature journaling. He teaches adults and children the discipline of observing along with the skills of drawing and painting. His website is johnmuirlaws.com.

There is an abundance of beautifully illustrated picture books about nature, inspiring kids of all ages. Each nature topic in this book has suggestions. Scan the nonfiction picture book section at your local library for more.

A field guide is essential for identifying things found outside. Audubon guides are books with full-color photographs arranged in categories that make pinpointing your specimen quick and sure. For a digital option, there are several smartphone apps that identify specimens from pictures you take. Each topic in this book has the coordinating field guides or notable digital resources listed.

Birds

Birds

All birds have feathers, a beak, and a lightweight skeleton with vertebrae. They are warm-blooded and reproduce by laying hard-shelled eggs. Most fly, but there are exceptions, like the penguin and the ostrich.

Birds that stay in a region all year long are called nonmigratory birds. Those that travel with the changing seasons are classified as migratory birds. Primarily, these birds move south for the winter as their food sources diminish in colder regions. They return north for preferred nesting locations in the spring/summer.

Field Guides:

National Audubon Society Field Guide to Birds: Eastern Region (Choose if your area)

National Audubon Society Field Guide to Birds: Western Region (Choose if your area)

Merlin Bird App

allaboutbirds.org

Books (Available free on archive.org):

A First Look at Birds by Millicent Selsam

Crinkleroot's Guide to Knowing the Birds by Jim Arnosky

Egg to Chick by Millicent Selsam

A First Look at Owls, Eagles, and Other Hunters of the Sky by Millicent Selsam

Owls by Herbert Zim

Study 12

Become familiar with 12 different types of birds in your area

Get to know the local birds by studying a new one each week for 12 weeks. Birds are watchful, fast, and may take flight at any moment. When you spot one, everyone in your group should quietly say aloud what they notice about the appearance: "black feathers," "black beak," "red and yellow patches on the tops of the wings," "about the size of a robin," "in a large group." This will help you remember the features when you look the bird up in your digital or print field guide.

Draw the bird in your nature journal and label it with its name. Look at the picture in the field guide if necessary to capture the details. Write about what you observe.

Birdwatch

Practice observing patiently and quietly, learn to use binoculars, notice everything you can

Sit quietly in a nature area and birdwatch. Use binoculars to see them better. While looking at the bird, slowly raise the binoculars to your eyes. Do not make any sudden movements, which may startle the bird. Pay attention to the bird's appearance and behavior.

After observing, pull out your nature journals and record everything you can about the bird. If it does not stick around, you could draw it from the field guide picture.

- Where did you see the bird? Why was it there?
- What was the bird doing? How did it move?
- If you hear its call, write what it sounds like. What would it have "said" if put into words?
- Was it alone or in a flock?
- If the bird was in a group, how did they interact? Were they all the same kind?
- Did the bird seem to be on the lookout for danger? How so?
- What made the bird leave? Where did it go?

Flight Patterns

Practice quiet watchfulness, consider how birds fly, identify bird names, compare bird flight patterns by type

Bring a blanket and lie flat on your back in the middle of an area popular with birds, such as a forest, meadow, or riverside. Be quiet and patient, watching for birds to fly above. Tell your group to say aloud their observations as birds pass. Then write the bird's name, draw a simple sketch of the bird's flight path in their nature journals, and write notes about anything that was unique.

For each bird:

- What kind is it?

- Does the bird fly up and down in the air like going over hills, swerve side to side, or travel in a straight line?

Bird Flight Patterns

Bird Type	Flight Pattern	Notes

- Was the bird flying by itself, with a flock in a group formation, or in a cluster?

- Is it flapping its wings quickly, slowly, or not at all (soaring)?

- Are the wings straight out or swept backward?

- Does the bird sing or call while flying?

- Do all birds of the same kind fly the same way?

- Can you tell where the bird was going? Where was it coming from?

Diagram a Bird

Get to know the anatomy of a bird

Look carefully at a bird and draw it carefully in your nature journal. Label the parts: bill, eye, ear patch, crown, chin, throat, breast, thigh, tarsus (leg), foot, wing, and tail. For students who want to go into more detail, each section of feathers has a specific name and can be diagrammed using an online or print reference.

Bird Feeder Guestbook

Attract backyard birds, recognize common birds, observe birds up close, consider the food types that different types of birds eat, record data in a chart

Hang a bird feeder in a spot that you can easily see from inside and keep a "guestbook" of its visitors. This could be done in any season, though if you have cold winters, the bird population may be higher in your area in the spring/summer/fall. Your list could be kept on an open nature journal page or a clipboard placed near the window. Supply your viewing spot with a means of identifying the birds, such as a bird field guide or bird app.

Each bird type is attracted to a specific kind of food: seed, suet, fruit, nuts, or nectar. Hang multiple feeder types to attract the widest variety of visitors.

In your guestbook, list: bird name, time of day it visits, season it is around, and type of food it likes. Some birds prefer to eat seeds that have fallen on the ground, while others take directly from the feeder. Write this down too.

Bird Feeder Guestbook

Bird Type	Time of Day It Visits	Season	Food It Eats

It may take time for birds to find your feeder, but you will get to know the neighborhood birds well once they do.

- For birds who like seeds, where do they get these in the wild? (Plants and grasses)
- Suet cakes purchased from the store contain fat and usually a combination of seeds, grains, fruits, nuts, dried insects, and eggshells. Where do they get these in the wild? (Fat from dead animals, seeds and grains from plants, fruits and nuts from trees, live insects from the ground, eggshells from nests)
- Where do birds find fruit and nuts in the wild? (Plants and trees)
- Where do nectar-loving birds find their food in the wild? (Flowers on plants, shrubs, trees, and vines)

Wren House

Make a connection with wrens, learn how wrens nest and care for their young, hear baby birds chirp, watch baby birds fledge

Background: Wrens are one of the most common backyard birds and are found throughout the United States. They live in the southernmost parts during the winter then move to central and northern states to breed. They thrive in backyards, eagerly taking residence in birdhouses. They are creatures of habit. They return to the same spots to raise young, year after year. You cannot miss it when they arrive- their cheerful song is a welcome treat in the spring.

Activity: Invite a wren family to your backyard. Buy or construct a birdhouse. Many styles will work, but the opening needs to be 1 1/4" in diameter and no bigger. This will prevent other birds from entering and endangering the eggs/babies. Hang the home near a window visible from the breakfast table, if possible.

Document your wrens with a series of nature journal entries. Start with the date the birdhouse was hung and keep watch to note when wrens first discover it. Continue to add to your journal as you notice events over the next weeks. For each, list the date and then write what happened. Include drawings, diagrams, and counts when helpful.

Wren House

Date	Event	Sketch

The parents start by flying to and from the house, bringing nesting material. Once the eggs hatch, the parents switch to bringing all sorts of spiders and insects to feed their young. After some days, the babies can be heard chirping away and might be seen sticking their heads out of the door. After 2 or 3 weeks, the baby birds leave the nest in their first clumsy flight, called fledging.

Wrens may raise one brood or two. When the birds are gone, about midsummer, check out the nesting materials used. You might be surprised by what the birds chose. The house does not have to be cleaned out each year, as the wrens will prepare it next spring. You should expect your guests at about the same time each year.

- What date did the wrens start nesting? Did they raise one brood or two?
- Are both the female and the male involved in raising babies? Can you tell the male and female apart?
- How long does it take the parents to build the nest?
- What kinds of food do you see them bringing to the babies?
- When do the babies make noise? When are they quiet?
- What time of day did the babies fly from the nest for the first time? Did they look the same or different from their parents? Did they return to the nest? Did the parents?
- What materials did the birds use for the nest? How full was the house?

Bird Count

Notice birds in your area, practice identifying birds, collect and record information in a chart, analyze data to draw conclusions

Work together as a group to make a list of all the birds you see while on a nature hike. Have one person be the scribe while everyone else is on the lookout. When someone spots a bird, work together to identify it using a field guide or app. Write the bird's name down. Add tally marks for multiple bird sightings. At the end of your walk, look at the data collected and analyze what you found.

- Which kind of bird did you see most often?
- Why do you think you saw more of them?

Diagram a Feather

Learn about molting, identify each part of a feather

Background: Birds typically grow a whole new set of feathers every year, dropping old ones on the ground as fresh ones take their place. This process is called "molting" and happens over a few weeks. This gradual change ensures that the bird does not have any bald patches in the process. Molting takes a lot of energy so it usually happens before or after breeding and migrating.

Like human hair and animal fur, feathers are not living and they wear out. Once full-size, the feather cannot continue to grow or repair itself. Over time, the tips can become ragged, the color can fade in the sun, it can become brittle and lose fluffiness. Thus, new feathers are needed.

Many adult birds grow new feathers that match the color and pattern of their old feathers. In some species, juvenile birds change color and pattern as they mature. Others change from one coloring to another by season. This change happens when they molt. Your field guide may include the alternate appearances.

Activity: Find either a wing or a tail feather (instead of a small, fuzzy feather). Some birds are protected by law and their feathers cannot be taken home. Study it on-site or be sure it is allowed before you collect it.

- Draw and label the parts of the feather in your nature journal: calamus (tip where it connected to the bird's skin), rachis (central post), barbs (branches off the rachis), barbules (branches off the barbs).

- How do the barbs interlock to keep the feather's shape?

- Run your fingers up and down the feather. How does a bird preen its feathers with its beak?

- Feathers serve a lot of purposes for the bird. Look at the feather and describe how it does the following: Block the wind? Protect the bird from wetness? Catch the wind for flying?

Feather Study

Get to know the anatomy of a feather, understand the types of feathers and the purpose they serve

Background: Birds have seven different kinds of feathers. Each has a specific purpose. Tail feathers are fan-shaped and help with steering while flying. Asymmetrical wing feathers are stiff and windproof. Contour feathers are short and waterproof, covering the body like roof shingles for protection. Semiplume feathers are fluffier and closer to the body to keep the bird warm. Down feathers are the softest, warmest, and positioned closest to the bird's body. They have only a short central post (rachis) or none at all. Two other feather types look more like whiskers and are located on the bird's face: filoplumes and bristles.

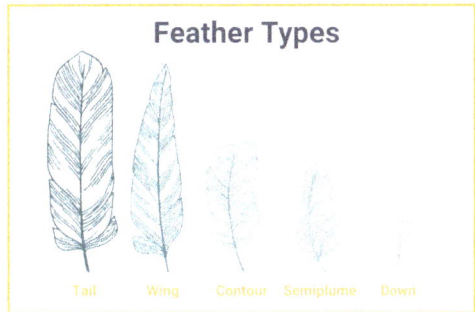

Feather Types

Tail   Wing   Contour   Semiplume   Down

Activity: Find a feather in nature and determine which kind it is. While closely examining it, draw it and write your observations in your nature journal.

- What type of feather do you have?
- What shape, color, and texture is the center part (called the rachis)?
- What shape, color, and texture are the barbs? Is there a pattern?
- Is the feather symmetrical?
- Look at it under a microscope to see the branching structure and tiny hooks. Can you describe how your feather is made up?
- What kind of bird is it from? An internet search may help.

Make a Nest

Make a bird nest, consider how birds use their bodies to make nests, simulate weather and test nest durability

Background: Birds build nests to protect their eggs and hatchlings. Their babies cannot escape or defend themselves for weeks yet are sought after by predators. These homes are camouflaged in the environment since they are made of local natural materials. The nest must shelter the babies from cold temperatures, wind, and rain.

Birds collect nearby materials like twigs, leaves, pine needles, mud, feathers, moss, dry grass, and man-made items stolen from backyards. Using their beak, wings, feet, and tail, they arrange and weave their findings into a cup shape, just large enough for their eggs.

Activity: Try making a nest. Walk around and gather many types of materials. These should be light enough for a bird to transport.

Form the bulk of the nest with a center cup. Strengthen it by weaving in longer strips of grass or twigs. You could reinforce the structure by painting it with mud and letting it dry in the sun. Line the inside of the nest with moss, feathers, or fluffy seed heads to make it soft and warm.

Draw the finished nest in your nature journal and write about how you constructed it.

- Which materials did you use? Is it possible for a bird to get and transport these? How?
- What materials are the easiest to shape: stiff or flexible?
- How does a bird construct a nest using only its beak, wings, feet, and tail? Watch an online video of a bird building a nest to see how they do it.

Next, test how well your nest is built. Write how well it performed in your nature journal.

- Wind: Hold the nest in the palm of your hand and wave it around. Did it stay together?
- Rain: Pour water into the nest. Does it drain or puddle?

Notice Nests

Examine bird nests, distinguish bird nests from squirrel nests

Background: Birds build and use nests in the spring, abandoning them when they have finished raising young. Just as birds are different sizes, so nests can be large, medium, or small. They may be built high up in a tree, laid directly on the ground, or even dug into a riverbank. Each type of bird has its preference. Squirrels also build nests. These are built high up in the branches of a tree with a disorderly concoction of dry leaves.

Activity: Walk through a nature area looking for nests. When you spot one, decide if it was made by a bird or a squirrel. Make notes in your nature journal, drawing a rough sketch, and add a description. If you see the owners, write that down too.

- How are squirrel nests and bird nests different?
- What materials were used to make the nest? Where did the bird get them? How were they carried there?
- Where is the nest located? Why do you think it chose that spot?

Dissect a Nest

Learn how birds make nests, identify materials that were incorporated, consider why the nest was made that way

Find an abandoned nest and examine it closely. Nests are unoccupied after birds have raised young— in late summer, fall, or winter. Draw the nest in your nature journal. Note how the bird built it to stay together.

Then, using tweezers, pick apart the nest and separate the material into piles. On your page, label the materials you see.

- Look around. Where did the bird get the materials for the nest?
- How many different materials were used?
- Is the outer part of the nest different from the inner part? Why was it made that way?
- How did the materials serve to camouflage the nest?

"Everybody needs beauty as well as bread, places to play in and pray in, where nature may heal and give strength to body and soul."

John Muir

Creek,
River,
Lake,
Ocean

Creek, River, Lake, Ocean

Our land is equipped with an efficient drainage and water storage system in the form of creeks, rivers, lakes, and oceans. When rains fall, the water flows through these bodies to keep our homes and lands dry. About a quarter of it is soaked up by the land and held underground in aquifers. These are like sponges, keeping water accessible to sustain our lives and homes.

The whole system is powered by gravity. Creeks flow downward into rivers and eventually out to the ocean, pooling up in lakes and ponds where the ground dips. Oceans lay at sea level, a lower elevation than the land we live on. Along the path, these waterways support an abundance of wildlife.

Books (Available free on archive.org):

Follow the Water from Brook to Ocean by Arthur Dorros

See Through the Lake by Millicent Selsam

See Along the Shore by Millicent Selsam

Rivers by Irving Adler

Trace Your Waterways

Follow water flowing from a source near your home out to the ocean, see how waterways work together, use a satellite view map, practice cardinal directions

Look at a map of your area on the internet and pinpoint your closest familiar waterway. This could be your neighborhood creek, the river you hike beside, or the lake beach where you go swimming. Using the satellite view, trace the waterway's path out to the ocean. You are going in the right direction if smaller rivers flow into larger ones. You may see creeks or rivers disappear under highways, but pop back up on the other side. Search the shorelines of lakes to find where the water comes in and where it flows back out.

In your nature journal, do a rough sketch of the path, labeling the major creeks, rivers, lakes, and the ocean. Put your home on the map.

The next time you visit your waterway, remind the children that, curving and turning, the water they see splashing by continues onward, all the way to the vast ocean.

- While looking at the waterway, which direction is the water going, North, South, East, or West?

- Imagine you are a bird and fly straight up from this spot and look down. Do you remember seeing this on the satellite map?

- Ask the students to point which direction you would have to fly to see some of the specific water bodies you discovered on your map. Which direction is the spot where this water will flow out to the ocean?

Make a Model

Understand how gravity affects water flow

Background: Water always flows downward. This is obvious with a waterfall but applies equally to the river that flows out from it. If the conditions change and the river meets a higher elevation, it puddles up to become a lake. It continues to rise until it has a downward path, then continues on its way. Rivers join with rivers, generally growing larger until they meet the ocean- the lowest elevation of all.

Activity: Have the child use a water-resistant clay like plastilina to make a model of a creek, river, lake, and ocean system. Shape the clay to be the banks and bottom of each. The creek should be small and flow into a larger river. Lakes should be wide and flat bottomed, with an inlet and an outlet. The ocean is the largest and at the end of the line. When water is poured in at the creek, it should flow through the system.

- How does the elevation of the ground (the clay) affect the flow of water? (Steeper downward creates a faster flow)

- If water gets stuck in your model, how could you fix it? (Adjust elevation)

- In nature, how could a river turn into a lake? (Sediment could raise the elevation and block the flow of water, creating a "bowl")

Supported Wildlife

Discover the variety of plants, animals, and insects that rely on a local waterbody

Background: Natural sources of water are important to wildlife. It is home for many fish, amphibians, insects, reptiles, and water plants. These we might notice while we are exploring, others we will not. Some animals use the water but live elsewhere. Trees that seem far off have reached the water underground with long roots.

Activity: Visit a local water body (creek, pond, wetlands, lake, etc.) Notice all the wildlife that relies on it for survival. As you walk around, look for examples from each of the nature study categories and write them down: amphibians, fish, birds, fungus, insects, spiders, invertebrates, mammals, reptiles, trees, and plants/wildflowers.

After building the list, consider other wildlife that may depend on the waterway, but were not spotted.

Water Samples

Collect and analyze samples, record data, formulate conclusions

Follow a creek or a river for some distance and collect water samples from several kinds of sites in jars. For example, dip into a fast-flowing section, a spot that puddles, a thin trickle, a wide flow, a place thick with plants, a shady area, and a sunny part. Label each jar with masking tape and a waterproof marker/pen. Let them settle.

In your nature journal, sketch a rough map and mark your sampled sites. Below, include an illustration for each sample and describe what it looks like. Formulate conclusions on why.

Water Samples

Map:

Sample 1
Location:
Description:

- How does the color compare in each sample?

- Which areas had the clearest water? Why?

- Which samples had sediment? What was it made of?

- If this was your only source of water, which spot would you drink from? What makes it the best option?

River Current

Compare/contrast fast-moving, slow-moving, and stagnant water

Visit a river or large creek that you can wade in. From the bank, have the children tell you everything they notice about the flow of water. Throw some sticks or leaves and watch them travel out of sight.

- Where is the water flowing fast? Where is it flowing slowly? Where is it completely still?

- Why do you think the water flows faster or slower in those areas? What makes water stop?

- Can you discern the water flowing downward along the river's path or does it look flat?

Allow them to safely step into the water and explore the swift water compared to the slow water.

- Is the depth the same or different?

- Are the bottoms the same or different?

- Does the temperature change?

On the shore, draw and write your findings in your nature journal. Sketch the section of the river you can see and label the fast-moving parts and the slow-moving parts.

Carrying Loads

Experiment with how water moves materials

Standing on a bridge or at the edge of a creek or river, allow the kids to throw things into the water and observe what happens.

- Which kinds of materials (rocks, sticks, leaves, dirt) float and are carried by the water? Which kinds sink?
- Does the water move faster in the middle of the river, toward the edges, or is it going at the same speed?
- If you throw a handful of sand in fast-moving water and another in slow water, which will carry the sand farther? Why?
- Do you see any shallow spots where the sand and rocks are dropped off by the water?
- What kinds of things is the water carrying along? Look upstream and see if you tell where it is picking up those items. If you see leaves passing by, can you see the tree they came from?

After experimenting, create a nature journal entry explaining how water moves materials.

Aquatic Plants

Examine plants that grow in the water, compare and contrast them to land-based plants

Examine a plant living in the water of a creek, pond, or lake. Identify it using a field guide, nature app, or internet search. Draw it in your nature journal, label it, and write what you notice.

- How many of these plants are growing nearby?
- Is the plant rooted in the dirt at the bottom of the water body or is it free-floating?
- How far from the shore do the plants grow? Why?
- Are the leaves submerged under the water, above the surface, or is it a mix?
- Are the leaves brittle or flexible? How do they compare to land plants?

- Look at a single leaf. Compare its top to its underside. How are they different?

- Place a water droplet on a leaf. What happens to it? Is the leaf absorbent or waterproof?

- Does the plant flower? Are the flowers above or below the water's surface? Why? Do you see any insects visiting them?

- How are aquatic plants similar to land plants? How are they different?

Aquifer Study

Learn about groundwater, research a topic on the internet, draw a map

Background: When it rains, droplets fall across the entire area. Some join the waters of creeks, rivers, lakes, and oceans as they splash the surface. Those that land on the ground moisten the soil for the grass, trees, and plants living there. Heavy rains saturate the topsoil until it cannot hold any more. The excess water either flows out to a waterway or drains into an underground aquifer. These are large areas of porous rocks and sands that soak up the water like a sponge.

A natural spring occurs when this groundwater re-emerges at the surface. Artificially, wells and pumps pull this water up to be used by homes, businesses, and farms. Aquifers are an important source of freshwater in addition to the waterways that we can see.

Activity: Find out where the closest underground aquifer is by researching it on the internet. Discover the type of rock it is. Visit a natural spring if there is one local. In your nature journal, draw or trace a map of your state and color in the major aquifers. Draw a symbol for your home.

- How do underground aquifers work?

- Where does your home drinking water come from?

- If you visited a natural spring, how was the water different from the water that comes from your kitchen faucet? How was it the same?

Ice Play

Experience a frozen creek, discover how ice forms and how it cracks

Visit a creek in the winter to experiment with ice. Dress warmly and wear waterproof boots and gloves. Make sure everyone stays on the land or ventures out onto the ice only when it is safe- where the depth is shallow or where the ice is frozen thick. Do a nature journal entry back at home with a drawing and description of what you discovered.

- As you approach the frozen water, see if you can tell how the ice forms: from the middle or the edges first? Why do you think that is?

- How would you describe the texture and color of the ice?

- Can you see any trapped air bubbles or things like sticks that are usually floating on the surface when the water is flowing? How did they get there? Can you tell if the water is still flowing under the ice?

- From land, break the surface of the water's edge with your boot or a rock if you can. Does it crack in predictable ways? Are the cracks straight lines, curvy lines, or a mix?

- Try to pick up ice chunks from different spots. Is the ice the same thickness everywhere?

- Slide things across the creek to the opposite bank (sticks, rocks, ice chunks, etc). Which materials slide better? Why? (The smoothest things have less friction and go faster and farther)

- Throw a heavy rock onto the ice. What does it sound like? Why? (The water underneath may resonate like a drum)

Tide Pools

Become familiar with plants and sea creatures in tide pools

Go to a rocky ocean coastline while the tide is out to examine the tide pools. These puddles on the rocks have trapped seawater with the plants and animals that dwell in it. Draw what you see in your nature journal. Use a microscope to examine closely.

- How many different things did you find? Did you see plants or animals or both?

- How did they get there?

- Did you see any wildlife feeding on the plants and animals trapped in the tide pools?

- What do you think will happen when the tide comes back in?

Fresh vs. Salt

Compare freshwater and saltwater, understand that saltwater is denser than freshwater

Compare samples of freshwater (taken from inland ponds, lakes, rivers) to ocean saltwater. If you don't live near an ocean, you can simulate it by heating 4 1/4 cups (1000 grams) of water and dissolving 2 Tablespoons (35 grams) of salt in it. With both samples at room temperature, analyze the similarities and differences. Write and illustrate your findings in your nature journal.

- How does each sample smell?

- Do the samples look the same or different?

- What does each sample feel like between your fingers?

- Why might some animals live in freshwater, but not survive in saltwater? Why might some need saltwater and die in freshwater?

Place several household objects in each sample to see if they sink or float. First, estimate what will happen.

- Why do some things float in both samples? (They are less dense than water)

- Why do some things sink in both samples? (They are denser than water)

- Why do some things sink in freshwater, but float in saltwater? (Since saltwater is denser than freshwater, the item's density is between these two)

"In all things of nature there is something of the marvelous."

Aristotle

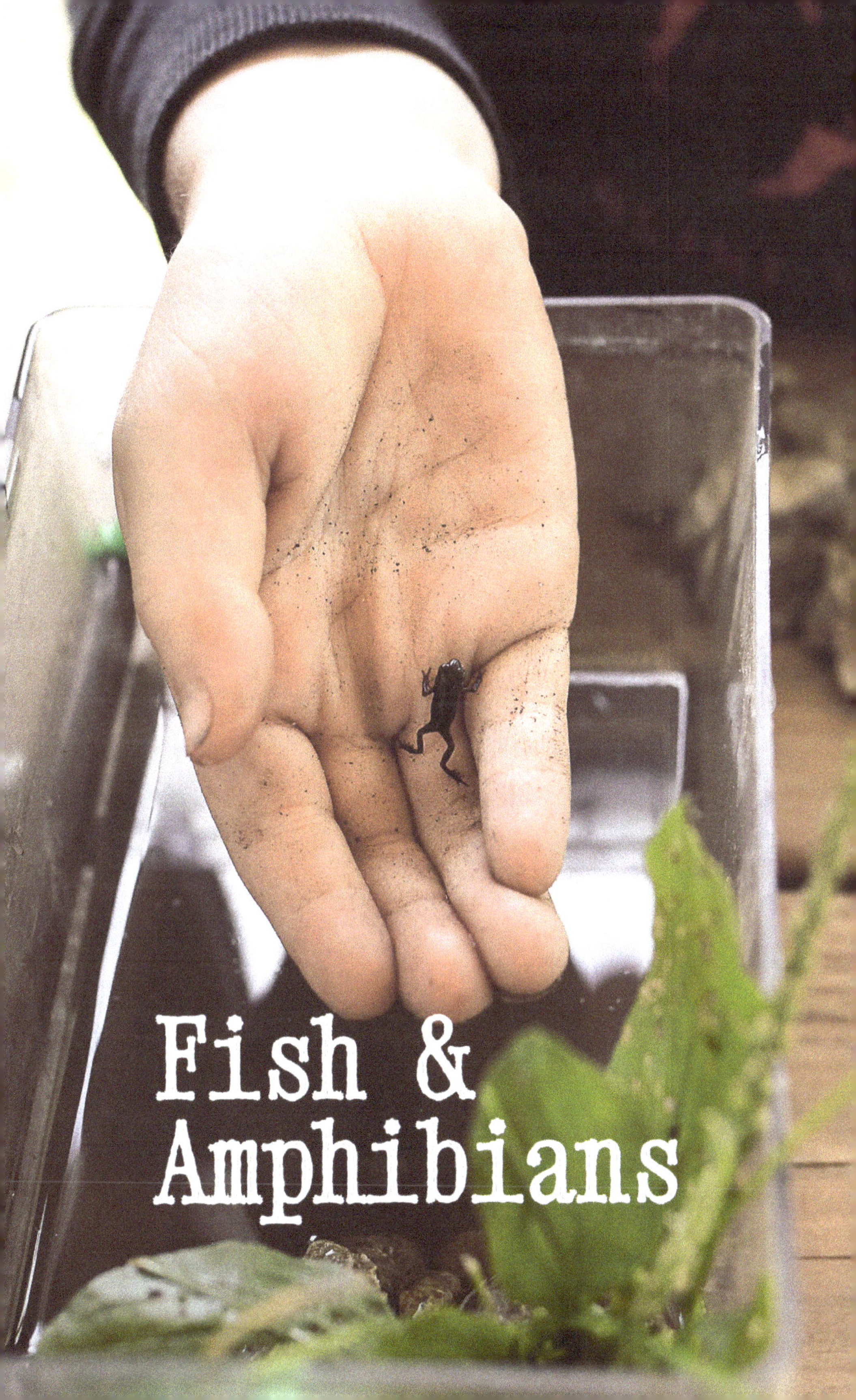

Fish & Amphibians

Fish and Amphibians

Fish live in water full-time and have a backbone. Most use gills to breathe and fins to move. There are thousands of varieties of fish, some of which thrive in freshwater and others in saltwater. A few species can live in either.

Amphibians include frogs, toads, and salamanders. The name "amphibian" comes from the Greek meaning "duel life". They live part of their lives on land and part in the water, changing dramatically through their life cycle (though there are a few exceptions). Most breathe both with their lungs and through their skin. They all have a backbone, are cold-blooded, and reproduce by laying eggs. You may best find them seeking out the sun when it is cool and shade when it is hot, as they use the environment to regulate their body temperature.

The best places to examine fish and amphibians in nature are in and around ponds, rivers, and lakes. To see those that are not native to your area, visit an aquarium.

Field Guides:

National Audubon Society Field Guide to Fishes

National Audubon Society Field Guide to Reptiles and Amphibians

National Audubon Society Field Guide to Tropical Marine Fishes

Books (Available free on archive.org):

Freshwater Fish and Fishing by Jim Arnosky

Hook, Line, and Seeker: A Beginner's Guide to Fishing, Boating, and Watching Water Wildlife by Jim Arnosky (This is a longer book)

The How and Why Wonder Book of Reptiles and Amphibians by Robert Mathewson

Frogs by Gail Gibbons

Frogs and Toads by Herbert Zim

Frogs and Polliwogs by Dorothy Childs Hogner

Go Fishing

Catch fish to learn about them

Catch a fish with a fishing pole and examine it carefully, finding out all you can about it. Ask an experienced fisherman to help if needed. Look at the fish from all angles. Keep it in a water-filled bucket to refer back to while you nature journal your observations. Draw, count, measure, and write about what you discover.

- How does the bait you used compare to what the fish eats naturally?
- How does the fish behave out of water compared to when it is in the water?
- In what ways are fish designed for swimming? Is it their body or their fins that primarily propels them through the water?
- Are the eyes on the sides or front of the fish? Why were they put there? Compare this to your eyes. What advantages does the placement give the fish?
- Examine the scales up close. How could you describe them?
- Examine the gills. How do they work?

Diagram a Fish

Get to know the anatomy of a fish

Look at a fish in a tank or catch one with a fishing pole and examine it to identify each part: eye, nares (nose), mouth, scales, gills, and fins: dorsal (back), caudal (tail), anal (belly), pelvic (chest), and pectoral (side). Draw and label these in your nature journal.

Fillet a Fish

Cut open a fish to learn about what is inside

Dissect a fish. Recruit the help of a fisherman if needed. Pull out each part and identify it if you can. If a real-life experience is impossible, search for a video dissection online. Record your findings in your nature journal.

- Which part of the fish do we eat? Is it a large or small part of the overall body?

- How large is the brain? Where is it located?

- Find the heart. How is it different from a human heart? How is it similar?

- What are fish bones like? How are they situated in the body?

- Cut off some scales and look at them under a microscope. How would you describe them? Do they remind you of anything?

Fish Patterns

Become aware of the colors and patterns of fish

As you visit an aquarium or go fishing, study the fish skin patterns. Mark squares in your nature journal and depict each fish's skin using accurate colors, illustrating one swatch per fish type. Identify the fish name using an app or field guide and label.

Fish Patterns

- What are the most common colors? Which colors are missing?

- What shapes do you see? Are they exactly the same all over the fish?

- Are fish shiny or dull? What makes them that way?

Salamander Study

Learn about salamander habitats, create a chart to compare salamanders to frogs and lizards

Background: Salamanders are found in most regions, except in desert or polar climates. They have characteristics somewhat between a frog and a lizard: smooth, wet skin like a frog, but long bodies with tails like a lizard. Some breathe with lungs, others with gills, and others only through their skin. Some have two legs; others have four. They have a variety of colors and patterns.

Activity: Encounter a salamander in the wild or at a nature center, zoo, or pet shop. Make three columns in your nature journal: "Like a frog," "Like a lizard" and "Unique to a salamander". List all the features you see under the corresponding categories.

Salamander Characteristics		
Like a Frog	Like a Lizard	Unique to a Salamander

For the best chance to find a salamander in the wild, look in forested areas with a water source. All live near water so they can keep their skin moist and most lay their eggs there. During the day, salamanders hide under rocks or up in trees. They are nocturnal and prefer cool temperatures. Since they are active at night, it may be easier to find one then. Use a glow stick or light to attract them.

Raise Tadpoles

Witness the development of a frog or toad

Care for tadpoles as they transform into frogs or toads, watching their development along the way. To find eggs or tadpoles, check ponds, lakes, and creeks in early spring. Eggs are jelly-like masses with dark centers floating in calm waters. Tadpoles swim around in groups near shore and are easily caught in a fine mesh net. Place them in a bucket or water-tight container to transport them home.

FISH AND AMPHIBIANS

Tadpoles need to be housed in an aquarium, plastic storage bin, or water-tight container. Fill it with a few inches/centimeters of untreated water, either from the source you found them in or with collected rainwater. Replace it when it becomes cloudy. Add a rock that rises above the water level. Once the tadpoles develop legs, they will climb onto it.

In nature, tadpoles feed on plants native to their habitat. An easy substitute is boiled spinach. Cook up a batch and freeze it. Twice a day, sprinkle a pinch into their habitat. After they develop both sets of feet, they will stop eating and instead digest their tail. Following that, they primarily eat insects. Since it is significantly harder to feed them, now is a good time to release them back into the environment where you found them. However, if you choose to keep them longer, pet shops sell live crickets that will sustain them.

Raising Tadpoles

Date:

Sketch:

Notes:

Create a dated log in your nature journal. Each day, write the date on the left side and include a sketch of your tadpoles. Write about what you notice.

- How do tadpoles swim?
- At what stage were you able to discern their eyes?
- How much did the body grow?
- Did the front legs or back legs appear first?
- How did the needs change over time?

Diagram a Frog

Get to know the anatomy of a frog

Catch a frog from a pond or creek and place it in a clear container to inspect it closely. Some types are slow enough to be captured by hand, while others may need the help of a fishing net. Look at your frog and point out the parts: eye, tympanum (ear), nares (nose), mouth, vocal sac, foreleg, hind leg, feet, and back. Draw and label the frog in your journal.

- What does the skin feel like? What colors/patterns do you see on it?

- In what ways are frogs designed for swimming?

- How are frogs able to jump so far compared to their size?

- Are the front and back feet identical or different? Some species have webbed feet just on the back legs, while others also have them on the front.

- How do webbed feet help the frog?

Tree Frog Calls

Recognize tree frog calls in your neighborhood, distinguish the sounds made by tree frogs from insects

Background: The mixed chorus of nature sounds on warm nights is put on primarily by insects and tree frogs. While mammals may call out at specific times, birds are mostly sleeping by nightfall and reptiles are quiet in general. Tree frogs, however, spend a lot of their time chirping and croaking during the breeding season. They are working to attract mates and communicate with each other. Since they live in trees, they can be hard to spot. If you are lucky, you might find one near your porch lights, hunting the bugs that congregate there.

Activity: Listen for tree frogs in the spring and summer. Research the types native to your area and get familiar with their calls through an internet search. When you go out at night to hear them firsthand, try to identify them by name. Write up who you heard in your nature journal.

- If you put the tree frog's call into words, what would you choose?

- Are you surprised that tree frog calls do not sound like the classic "ribbit"?

Make a Toad House

Observe a toad firsthand, understand its habitat needs

Background: Toads start as tadpoles in the water like frogs, but once fully grown, they typically spend the majority of their time on land. They need a water source nearby, but they are not as dependent on it as frogs. Since they feed on slugs, snails, and insects, toads are helpful in the garden.

Activity: Attract a toad to your garden by creating an ideal home. First, choose a spot under the leaves of a shady plant, which offers hiding and protection from their predators: birds, snakes, and house pets. Keep a shallow container or plate filled with water if a natural source is absent. Place a planter upside-down to provide a sturdy shelter that stays cool during the day. Terra cotta keeps out the heat best. Place it on stacked rocks and leave a gap for an entrance. If you use a plastic pot, cut a small doorway.

Wait some days for a toad to take up residence. If no one arrives, search for a toad in a wet woodland area amongst damp leaves and move it in.

Draw and write about your toad tenant in your nature journal, recording everything you notice.

- How does the habitat you constructed meet the needs of the toad?
- What time of day does your toad leave the house? When does he stay inside? Why?

Frog Watch

Practice watching patiently and quietly, notice everything you can

Visit a pond, river, or lake habitat to encounter frogs. They blend into their surroundings very well, so walk along the shore while looking for movement. Once you have identified that an area has frogs, slow your pace and try to spot them before they jump. Stop and watch them for as long as you can. Quietly say aloud everything you notice about their appearance and behavior. Identify the type in your field guide and create a nature journal entry. Draw the frog and its environment.

- Where did you find the frog: on land, in shallow water, or in deep water? Did it blend in? How?
- What was the frog doing? Was the frog active or still? When it moved, how fast was it? What made it want to go?

Temporary Frog/Toad Pet

Spend an extended amount of time with a fish or an amphibian, learn about its habitat needs

Catch a frog or a toad and keep it for a few days. This will give you more time to watch it and learn about it. Some species are protected, so check local laws first.

Fill a bucket, tub, or aquarium with water from its natural habitat and include a rock for it to climb above the water's surface. Enclose the habitat with a breathable top. Adult frogs and toads can go two weeks without food, but if you keep yours longer than that, purchase live crickets from a pet shop.

Draw the frog or toad in your nature journal and write about what you learn. When you are ready, return the "pet" to the same spot you found it.

- Does your pet seem content in its temporary home, or is it looking for a way out?
- When is your pet most active? When is it still?
- Where does your pet spend most of its time? Why?

Long-Term Fish/Amphibian Pet

Learn to care for all the needs of a fish or an amphibian

Adopt a goldfish, betta fish, frog, or salamander from the wild or from a pet shop to keep as a long-term pet. Some species are protected, so check local laws first.

Learn about its needs and build a suitable habitat that is as close to nature as possible. Draw and write about your pet in your nature journal. Keep it in the schoolroom to watch during breaks from other studies.

- What are your pet's habitat needs? How have you met them?
- How does it eat? How is the food you buy different from what it would find in nature?
- When does your pet sleep? What does it look like when it does?

Fungus

Fungus

Mushrooms, molds, and yeasts are examples of fungus. Some are so tiny we cannot see them, while others are unmistakable. They are not plants, nor animals, nor bacteria. They are unique to themselves. Fungi are an essential part of nature as they are responsible for breaking down organic matter. They can be found in soil and on decaying plants and trees.

Fungi are spread by microscopic spores, which are always traveling through the air. They will not germinate until they land in a moist environment. Once growing, they feed on plant or animal material around them.

While many kinds of mushrooms are cultivated to eat, there are many more found in the wild that are poisonous. Make sure your kids are aware and do not snack. Additionally, the chemicals that make some mushrooms toxic could be absorbed through the skin. Confirm that a mushroom is safe before you handle it.

Field Guide:

> *National Audubon Society Field Guide to Mushrooms*

Books (Available free on <u>archive.org</u>):

> *Molds and Fungi* by Buffy Silverman

> *Mushrooms* by Millicent Selsam

> *Fungi and Lichens* by Wendy Madgwick

Before and After Rain Hike

Discover that fungus thrives in moist environments

Background: Fungi, such as mushrooms and molds, release an incredible amount of spores every day. These are carried by the wind. When they land in a moist spot, the conditions are ideal for them to grow quickly. After a summer rainfall, the number of sprouted fungi is noticeably higher.

Activity: Hike a trail in a warm month right after it rains. In your nature journal, note the molds and mushrooms you come across, making a simple map with their locations. Hike the same trail after a dry spell and look for your prior findings. Describe how they have changed. They may be missing altogether!

- Why do you think there are more mushrooms and molds after wet weather? What happens to them in dry spells?
- Do mushrooms look different in wet conditions compared to dry?
- Are mushrooms and molds found in groups or individually? Why?

Mushroom Hunt

Become aware of the variety of mushrooms growing around you

Background: Mushrooms thrive in shady, moist environments. There are so many kinds that it is hard to recognize and know the names of them all. However, since they are spread by spores carried by the wind, many of the same types often grow in the same area, becoming recognizable to the watchful eye. Some mushrooms are toxic and should not be handled until identified as safe.

Activity: As you hike, be on the lookout for mushrooms on the ground or growing on trees. In your nature journal, draw each one, describe it, note what it was growing on, and record its measurement. Count or estimate the number of mushrooms nearby.

Mushrooms

Growing on:
Description:

Growing on:
Description:

- Do all mushrooms look similar or can be they be quite different? How can you tell it is a mushroom?
- Did you see many of the same kinds of mushrooms near each other? Why is this?

Diagram a Capped Mushroom

Get to know the anatomy of a mushroom that has a cap

Background: Mushrooms with caps grow from spores dropped by other mushrooms of the same kind. With moisture, they germinate on the ground and drop roots. It first develops into an egg-like shape, called a button. Then it erupts above ground, leaving a volva at its base. It grows taller on a stalk until it breaks open a second time to spread its cap, leaving a ring (called an annulus) on the stalk. The mushroom then produces spores of its own from its downward-pointing gills, pores, ridges, or teeth, depending on the variety.

Activity: Find a mushroom on the ground and examine it carefully. Draw it in your nature journal and diagram the parts: cap (top), gills/pores/ridges/teeth (textured underside, gills are most common), spores, stalk, annulus (ring on the stalk), volva (base), and mycelium (roots). Not all parts may be visible on your specimen; label the parts you see.

Spore Print

Visualize how capped mushrooms spread via spores

Background: Mushrooms spread by releasing an uncountable number of spores every day. These microscopic "seeds" fall to the ground or float in the air. Very few will find the right conditions of moisture and warmth to germinate into a full mushroom. Those that do not immediately land in a suitable spot remain viable for a long time.

Activity: Find a capped mushroom and identify it to make sure it is safe to handle. Pluck it and cut off the stem. If it has a white underside, place it on a dark piece of paper. If it has a dark underside, place it on a white piece of paper. Set an upside-down jar over it to protect it from wind and moisture. Check it the following day to see what happened.

If a dust-like substance is found beneath, they are thousands of tiny spores. Mycologists (scientists who study fungi) use spore prints as one factor in identifying mushrooms.

If there is nothing below, the mushroom could be either too young or too old to produce spores. Also, a mushroom collected at a higher elevation may not drop its spores when brought lower.

Describe the color, shape, and quantity of the print in your nature journal, illustrating the parent mushroom and the spore print it made. Try to look at the spores under a microscope or magnifying glass.

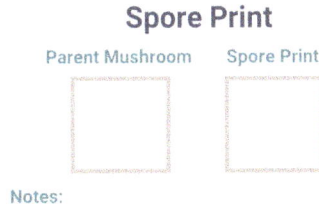

Spore Print

Parent Mushroom   Spore Print

Notes:

- Considering where they fell, where did the spores come from? (From under the cap)

- How big is one spore? Can you see it? Is it light enough to be carried by the wind?

- How many new mushrooms could be produced by this one you picked?

Dead Log

See how fungus aids decomposition

Background: Fungus is one of nature's chief recyclers, helping to break down decaying plant and animal materials. It has many forms, as recognizable mushrooms or as a hazy web, for example. As the fungus feeds, the host becomes soft and crumbly.

Activity: Find a dead log and examine it to see how many types of fungi you can find. Sketch and color or paint examples in your nature journal. Use a field guide or app to identify the fungus type.

- Where is the fungus growing on the log: top, sides, under, inside, all around?

- Is the environment wet or dry? Shady or sunny? How does this affect fungi?

- Is there just one kind of fungus or several? What kinds?

Puffball Study

Recognize puffball mushrooms in nature, understand how they spread their spores

Background: Puffball mushrooms look and operate a bit differently than capped mushrooms. Instead of the classic umbrella shape, these mushrooms are rounded, like a hot air balloon with its spores are stored inside. They may have a short stalk or none at all. When "popped" by animals, heavy raindrops, or passing kids, they release their spores in a smoky cloud.

Activity: Be on the lookout for puffball mushrooms on decaying logs or directly on the ground in meadows and forests. There are several varieties that can be as small as a golf ball or as large as a watermelon.

Popping these are fun for people of all ages, but stop and investigate it closely first. Draw it in your nature journal. Measure it and record everything you notice about it.

- What was the puffball growing on?
- How many are growing nearby?

Pop one with a stick and watch what happens. Describe it in your nature journal entry.

- What color is the haze that floats out? How does the haze dissipate?
- If there are multiple puffballs, does it seem like they all have the same amount of spores released when popped, or does mushroom size make a difference?

Bread Yeast

Understand how yeast makes bread fluffy, know that yeast is a fungus, see how fungus can remain dormant and then activate when conditions are right

Background: The yeast we use in baking is a fungus. The kind we buy at the store has been grown and then dehydrated so that it is dormant. When we add it to bread ingredients, it is "awakened" and starts feeding and multiplying. The moisture and the warmth rehydrate the yeast and it feeds on the sugars in the flour. As it does so, it releases "burps" of air bubbles that are trapped in the dough. This causes the dough to "rise," growing larger and less dense. When baked, the yeast is killed, leaving the fluffy, cratered texture we enjoy.

Activity: As you make homemade bread, write notes in your nature journal about what happens to the yeast in each step.

- Examine the yeast from the packet. What does it look like? Smell like?
- How does the recipe create the ideal environment of warmth, moisture, and food for the yeast?
- While the bread is rising, measure it periodically to see its growth.
- After the bread is baked, cut a slice and look closely at the surface. How were these air pockets created by the yeast?

For an additional experiment, trying baking bread with all the same ingredients except the yeast to see what happens.

Lichen List

Learn about lichen, categorize data, recognize lichen in its various forms

Background: Lichen is a partnership between fungus and algae that grows on the surfaces of rocks, soil, and trees. It is actually two organisms living together as one. They do not harm or feed on their host. They live on it to access sunlight as they use photosynthesis like plants. Lichen has many different forms, depending on the variety.

Activity: Look for lichens while hiking and record the different types you find. In your nature journal, draw and describe each specimen you encounter. There are thousands of species, so do not worry about learning the specific names, unless you are especially curious about them. Note what the lichen was growing on and where. Peel some off and look at it closely from all angles. Categorize it as one of the following types:

Fruticose- like a mini shrub

Foliose- flat leaf-like

Crustose- a crust or paint-like layer

Squamulose- scales with loose tips

Leprose- powdered

Gelatinous- jelly-like

Filamentous- hairy

Byssoid- wispy

Structureless

Lichen

Growing on:
Type:
Description:

Growing on:
Type:
Description:

- What is the most common type of lichen in this area?

- What colors and shades can lichen be?

- Lichen uses photosynthesis to generate food. Were they growing in the best places to receive sunlight?

- Lichen is very sensitive to air pollution. If it is growing abundantly, that is an indication of healthy air. If scarce, it could signify a problem. How many lichens did you see?

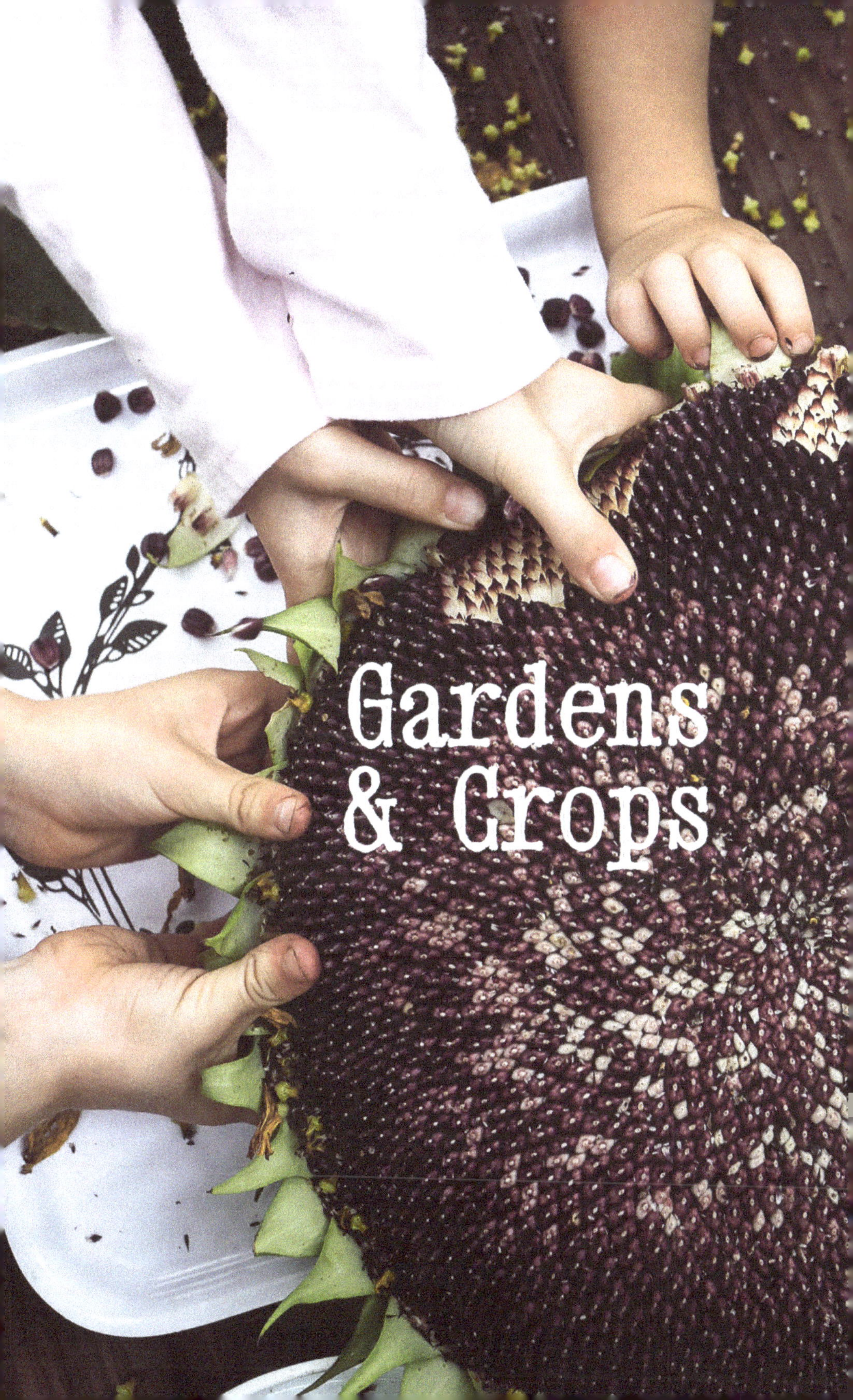
Gardens
& Crops

Gardens and Crops

Cultivating plants is a practice as old as humanity. We have always tended crops in order to harvest them for food, medicine, or simple enjoyment. While plants produce naturally, human effort increases their abundance and quality through improving the soil, watering, weeding, harvesting, and replanting.

Garden fruits and vegetables, cultivated flowers, and farmed crops have similar needs to each other, but at various levels. This includes sunlight, water, warmth, nutrients, soil, space, air, and protection from pests. Gardeners and farmers need only provide these and nature thrives to bless them with an abundant harvest.

Books (Available free on archive.org):

Roots, Shoots, Buckets and Boots by Sharon Lovejoy

Eat the Fruit, Plant the Seed by Millicent Selsam

Play with Plants by Millicent Selsam

From Seed to Plant by Gail Gibbons

The Hidden Magic of Seeds by Dorothy Edwards Shuttlesworth

Bits that Grow Big: Where Plants Come From by Irma Webber

The Vegetables We Eat by Gail Gibbons

The Tomato and Other Fruit Vegetables by Millicent Selsam

The Apple and Other Fruits by Millicent Selsam

Good Bugs and Bad Bugs in Your Garden: Backyard Ecology by Dorothy Childs Hogner

Study 12

Learn about 12 different kinds of garden plants/crops

Choose a new garden vegetable, fruit, flower, or plant from your yard to learn about each week for 12 weeks. Draw it in your nature journal. Identify the name, write your observations, and number what can be measured and counted. Be sure to include the part we eat and the parts we do not.

- Which parts are used by us? What are they used for?
- When is it ready for harvesting?
- Do you see any insects or disease that is hurting the plant? What can be done to help it?

Create a Menu

Classify garden plants by their major types, recognize plants as they are growing, identify the edible part

Visit a fruit and vegetable garden and write up a menu of produce. Organize a page in your nature journal with sections by the part of the plant we eat: Fruit, Flower, Seed, Leaf, Stem, Bulb, and Root/Tuber.

Garden Plants We Eat

Fruit	Flower	Seed	Leaf

Stem	Bulb	Root/Tuber

As you look at each plant, identify what it is and list it in the category for the part we eat. Tomatoes, for example, would be listed under "Fruit." Corn would be listed in the "Seed" slot. Bulb and Root/Tubers are harder to recognize since the edible part is under the soil line, invisible. Kids may be surprised to see what the foods they enjoy look like as they are growing.

Illustrate the menu with drawings and diagrams of plants as well as written descriptions of things you notice.

If you do not have a garden of your own, ask around to see if you could visit one kept by a friend. Avid gardeners typically love to show their growing space to interested people and would help identify the plants. Ask them to give the students time and space to discover for themselves first. If you cannot locate a home garden, you may have a community garden in your area.

- Looking at your list, which fruits and vegetables do you enjoy most? Are they fruits, flowers, seeds, leaves, stems, bulbs, or roots/tubers?

- What is similar about the plants in the same categories: Fruits? Flowers? Seeds? Leaves? Stems? Bulbs? Roots/Tubers?

Dissect Groceries

Think about familiar fruits and vegetables as plants, practice dissection, use a knife with precision

Background: Before fruits and vegetables were placed on the shelves of your local grocery store, they were grown on a farm. They were a full plant- complete with roots, a stem, leaves, flowers, fruit, and seeds. Many of these parts have been removed. The produce has been cleaned and packaged in some way to make it appetizing and easy to transport.

Activity: Take a fruit or vegetable out of your refrigerator and analyze it. Carefully cut it open and see what is inside. Draw what you see and write about it in your nature journal.

This project could be done with a new type each week over the semester. You could also do this activity when inclement weather makes going outside difficult.

- Which parts of the plant do you have: fruits, flowers, seeds, leaves, stems, bulbs, or roots/tubers? Which parts do you eat? Which parts do we throw away? Why?

- Describe the textures you notice. Does the outside feel different from the inside? If so, why were they were designed that way?

- Many edible plants need a lot of water when they are growing. Do you feel any moisture? What happens to the water inside the plant? Does it taste like water?

See-Through Planter

Watch seeds germinate, understand how plants sense gravity to send out their roots and shoots

Background: When conditions are just right, a plant emerges from its seed with one set of leaves, thin roots, and energy- everything it needs to start growing. This energy was stored in the seed when it was created by the mother plant. If the environment is favorable, it will grow into a mature plant.

Activity: Germinate seeds indoors using a see-through planter. You can purchase one or use a clear jar. Fill the container with soil and plant the seed against the glass just below the surface. Moisten with water and set it in a place where you can monitor it. If the soil dries out, add more water, but do not let the soil get wet and soggy. This may cause the seed to rot. The soil should feel like a damp sponge. As the days pass, you will be able to watch the seed swell, break free from its seed coat, drop roots, and raise its initial leaves using just the nutrition and energy stored in itself. This process happens over and over in cultivated gardens and in the wild.

In your nature journal, document the germination process in a comic strip format. In the first frame, draw the seed and write the date it was planted. Check on it each day. When you notice something new, add a frame with a drawing and the date.

Growing Plant Log

Date	Event	Height	Sketch

- Which emerged first, the root or the shoot?

- How do you think the plant knew to send the roots down and the leaves up? (They can sense gravity) You could turn it upside down in the planter and watch how it corrects itself.

- What does a seed need in order to germinate and sprout? (Moisture, warmth, light, oxygen)

GARDENS AND CROPS

Plant a Plant

Understand how plants grow, identify plant needs

Plant seeds and track their growth. Lettuce, pumpkins, and sunflowers grow quickly and vigorously in the ground. Marigolds, peas, and radishes grow fast and do well in pots. Plant several seeds, as some may not germinate.

Have an older child read about the plant's needs and take ownership to tend it. The back of the seed packet has the essential information. Younger children may need guidance, but allow them to do as much as possible. If the planting fails, guide them to figure out why and try again.

Track the progress in your nature journal or a dedicated garden journal. Format the page as a log, including the date, description of what happened, and an illustration. Once sprouted, use a measuring tape to track and record the height.

Plant Race

Compare the germination and growth rates of different types of plants, measure and collect data

Choose three different kinds of seeds to germinate indoors. Pumpkins, radishes, peas, and sunflowers spring up quickly and are easy to care for. Follow the directions on the packet.

In your nature journal, write down the date the seeds were planted. As each one sprouts, record how many days it took, draw it, and write what happened. When all have germinated, label the page with first, second, third place awards.

Plant Race

Date:

Plant: Plant: Plant:

Days to Sprout:
Place:

- Do all plants germinate at the same rate?

- How were the first leaves different from the leaves that appeared afterward? (These initial leaves are called "cotyledons" or "seed leaves". They are sprouted directly from the seed. The plant used these to make enough energy to produce leaves of their own, called "true leaves".)

Diagram a Plant

Get to know the anatomy of a plant

Visit a backyard garden or a field with a local crop. Look closely at a single plant. Identify it and draw it in your nature journal. If visible, show and label the fruit, flower, seed, leaf, stem, and root. Write notes of what you observe. You could do this activity for a new plant each week over the course of the term/semester.

Local Crops

Get to know which agricultural crops are produced in your area, learn about what goes into growing plants on a commercial scale

Learn which crops your area produces and visit the farms/orchards/ greenhouses to see them up close. Draw and describe the crop as a whole and identify the parts that are harvested, recording what you discover in your nature journal. Learn the start to finish process by talking to the farmer or researching on the internet. See if you can visit the place they are processed.

- Are most farmers in your area big companies or family-owned operations?

- What kind of tools and machines are needed?

- What are the threats to the crop: weather, pests, disease?

- What conditions make a good growing year or a bad year?

- What season are the crops harvested? What are the current prices for the crop?

Weeds

Become familiar with common weeds in your area

Background: A weed is just a plant in a place you do not want it. Those we label "weeds" are usually very good at propagating themselves and are hardy, growing well in many conditions. These qualities are why they pester our gardens and lawns.

Activity: Search your lawn or garden for weeds and make a list of them in your nature journal. Sketch each weed and identify it using a plant app or wildflower field guide. If it is not listed, try searching a description of it online. In reading about the weed, you may discover how it has been used in the past for medicine, dyes, improving the soil, or even food.

- Pinch the weed's stem close to the ground and pull up, trying to get the whole plant with the roots. Most weeds will easily regenerate leaves if the roots are still in the ground. Is this kind easy to remove or does it have to be dug out?

- Look closely at its root structure. Is there a thick central root? This is called a taproot and grows similarly to a carrot. Instead, is there a tangled web of equal-sized roots that cling to the soil?

- Does the weed grow tall and bushy or flat along the ground? How many leaves does it produce? How does this design help the plant to flourish?

- What do the weed flowers look like? Where are the seeds? How do they spread?

- Do you see many of these same weeds in this area?

- How might the weeds affect the grass and plants you want to grow here?

Propagate Moss

Learn about how moss is structured, watch moss grow

Background: Moss may be mistaken for a fungus, but it is actually a plant. They have tiny leaves and thrive in moist, shady environments.

Activity: Find moss in the forest. Look especially at the base of trees. Dig up a small part along with some extra soil. Place the moss in a container or on bare ground in a shady spot in your yard, mimicking its native environment. Moss is the perfect addition to a fairy woodland garden.

Water the moss whenever the soil feels dry. Measure the original piece and watch it day by day, recording in your nature journal as it changes, spreads, or dies.

- Look underneath the moss. Does it have roots?

- Can you discern leaves? How are these unlike leaves from wildflowers and trees? How are they similar?

- New moss plants are created both by sending out new shoots and by releasing spores from the tips of thin stems. Do you see spores on your plant? If not, it may not have any at this time. If your moss spreads, can you tell how it did so?

"Nature is rude and incomprehensible at first,

Be not discouraged, keep on, there are divine things well envelop'd,

I swear to you there are divine things more beautiful than words can tell.."

Walt Whitman
"Song of the Open Road"

Insects & Spiders

Insects and Spiders

There are more insects on Earth than any other kind of creature. This diverse group includes ants, butterflies, beetles, grasshoppers, bees, and water bugs. However, not all small crawly things are insects. The word "insect" comes from the idea of being "in sections"; every insect has a body made up of three parts: head, thorax, and abdomen. They also have six legs and two antennae. Their skeleton is on the outside of their body; they do not have vertebrae.

Spiders are not insects. They have a two-part body, eight legs, and no antennae. They live in similar habitats, however, and can be studied together.

For close observation, catch insects and spiders between a jar and its lid, quickly sealing the container. Some bite, so take caution. Kids can get close to bees, but should not trap them.

Field Guides:

National Audubon Society Field Guide to Insects and Spiders

National Audubon Society Field Guide to Butterflies

Books (Available free on archive.org):

The How and Why Wonder Book of Insects by Ronald Rood

Backyard Insects by Millicent Selsam

Where Do They Go? Insects in Winter by Millicent Selsam

A First Look at Spiders by Millicent Selsam

Spiders by Dorothy Childs Hogner

Questions and Answers About Ants by Millicent Selsam

The How and Why Wonder Book of Ants and Bees by Ronald Rood

The How and Why Wonder Book of Butterflies and Moths by Ronald Rood

Moths by Dorothy Childs Hogner

Insect/Spider Watch

Practice watching patiently and quietly, notice everything you can

Find an insect or spider outside and watch it carefully without interfering with it. Look for them on the leaves of plants, under logs, or in the soil. Say aloud what you notice about its appearance and behavior. Identify it in your field guide, draw it, and write about it in your journal.

- Where was it? Why was it there? What made it leave?
- What was it doing? How did it move?
- How many body segments does it have? How many legs? Is it an insect or spider? Is its body shiny or dull?

Study 12

Become familiar with 12 different kinds of insects/spiders

In this project, identify and observe 12 types of insects or spiders, studying one per week. These little creatures are everywhere, so you could head to a nature trail or park to find one, but your own backyard will do as well.

Each person should have a small container to catch and observe their finds. You could use a dedicated bug cage or a jar. Poke tiny holes in the jar lid or secure a piece of screen with the jar ring. When you spot an insect or spider, quickly plop the container upside down over them. Slide the top carefully underneath the creature and close it. Caution kids to encounter bees from a distance.

Study the insect or spider closely, looking at it from all angles. Identify it using a field guide, a phone app, or an internet search. Record your findings in a nature journal using pictures, words, and numbers to capture as much information as possible.

- Is it an insect or a spider?
- Where was it found? Why was it there?
- Was it by itself or in a group?

Adopt an Insect/Spider Pet

Observe an insect or spider for several days

Catch an insect or spider and have the child learn about its needs: habitat, water, food, and temperature. Build a suitable home in a bug cage, fishbowl, or jar and keep the new "pet."

Some will only eat live insects. Your porch light may be a good place to catch live bugs, as many are drawn to the light in the evening. Trap flying insects by clapping them between the open mouth of a jar and a stiff piece of cardboard. Place this whole container on its side in your bug habitat, giving you a little time to shut the habitat's cover before it flies out.

Write in your nature journal about your pet. You could make it a goal to keep a new pet every week for the term/semester or care for creatures as you happen to come across them in nature.

- How is your habitat different from the spot you found the insect/spider? What is similar?
- How does your pet eat its food?
- Does your pet do anything to make the habitat its own?

Diagram an Ant

Get to know the anatomy of an ant, use a magnifying glass

Capture an ant in a clear container and look at it closely using a magnifying glass. Draw and diagram its parts in your nature journal: head, antenna, mouth, mandible (jaws/pinchers), petiole (neck), thorax (middle body segment), abdomen (last body segment), and jointed legs. Some male ants and the queen grow wings during mating season. Label these if yours has them.

Ant Baby Rescue

Learn what ant babies look like, observe how ants care for their babies when they feel threatened

Background: Ant babies are small white sacs in the egg and larva stages. You may be able to see the dark ant inside or it may appear all white. The queen lays the eggs and other ants feed and care for these babies until they emerge as mature ants. Most insect parents die or leave after laying their eggs.

Activity: Quickly overturn rocks and stumps, looking for an ant colony living beneath. Scan for babies and notice what the adult ants do with them. Keep in mind that some ants bite, so avoid touching them. Write about what you saw in your nature journal.

- What do ants do when they feel threatened? Where did they go?
- How do adult ants move baby ants? Can babies move themselves?
- How quickly was the entire colony transported to safety?

Ant Buffet

Discover what food ants eat, experiment with what foods ants prefer, watch ants discover a food source and alert others from their colony

Background: Ants are foragers and omnivores, eating pretty much whatever they come across. This includes the same kind of food we eat, as well as the sap of plants, dead animals, and even other kinds of ants.

Activity: Set out several kinds of food near an ant colony outside to experiment with what they prefer. Options should be diverse, such as a dot of honey, a dead worm, a slice of fruit, flour, sugar, salt, an uncooked noodle, and a piece of hotdog. Draw each item in your journal, write about what happens, and estimate the number of ants that chose it.

- How long did it take for an ant to discover your feast? How did it find it?

- What did the first ant do once it found the food? How long before it went back to the colony? Did many ants from the colony start coming?

- Are the ants eating the food? Are they carrying it back to their home? How much can one ant carry? Do they work together? What are they doing with the big pieces?

- Did the ants seem to have a food preference? Which foods did they avoid?

Diagram a Spider

Get to know the anatomy of a spider

Catch a spider in an overturned jar so you can observe it closely. Use caution- some spiders bite. Draw the spider and label all the parts: cephalothorax (fused head and body), abdomen, jointed legs, eyes, chelicerae (fangs or jaws), pedipalps (front pinchers), and spinnerets (located at the bottom tip of the abdomen, used for making silk for webs).

Web Hunt

Discover the unique styles of webs that spiders make, watch spiders in nature

Background: Not all spiders spin webs, but many do. Their constructions can be seen in forests and on undisturbed buildings. Webs trap prey, entangling unsuspecting insects in the sticky strands as they pass by. Some spiders also use webs to protect their eggs or travel from one spot to another.

Activity: Explore a nature area in the spring, summer, or fall to look for spider webs. Be sure to check under the eaves of buildings, on low branches of trees, between the stems of close-growing ground plants, and on the ground.

You may encounter the most common types of webs: orb webs, sheet webs, and funnel webs.

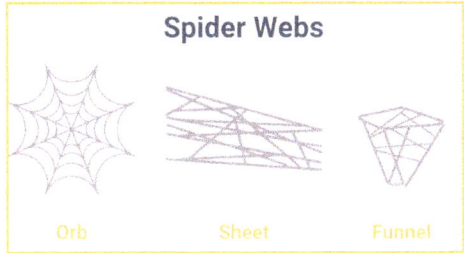

Spider Webs

Orb   Sheet   Funnel

Document the web sightings in your nature journal with drawings, measurements, and written notes.

For each web:

- Which kind of web is this?
- Do you see any prey trapped on the web? What kinds of insects were they? How were they stuck to the web?
- Do you see any egg sacs? What do they look like? Where on the web are they located?
- Do you see the spider on the web? Identify it in your field guide. What was it doing? If not around, where do you think it was?
- If the spider was working on the web, look closely. Where is the silk coming from? How does the spider arrange it?

About webs in general:

- Which web design seems to be the largest? Which is the smallest?
- What kinds of locations did you find orb webs? Sheet webs? Funnel webs? What does each web type need nearby for support?

Web Demonstration

Understand how spider webs are made and how they work

Background: Spider webs are made of silk spun inside the spider's body then drawn out and arranged using their legs. Most spiders can make multiple kinds of silk, varying in characteristics such as stretchiness, stickiness, and strength.

Activity: Find a web and examine it carefully. Make a nature journal entry with what you notice.

- Use a magnifying glass. What color is the silk that makes up the web? What is the texture?

- What is the shape of the overall web? What shapes do the threads make when joined together? Are they consistently the same shape, random, or somewhat in between? Do the threads make curves or straight lines?

- Does the web look finished or is it still in process?

Webs are often used to capture prey, entangling unsuspecting insects. Test how this happens using a small piece of leaf. Gently touch the web and then simulate an insect trying to get free by wiggling, using only the strength of a bug.

- What happened to the web when the leaf came in contact with it?

- Touch the web with your fingers. What does it feel like? Does it stick to you?

- Why do you think webs are designed as they are: almost see-through, sticky, and relatively strong for their size?

Fireflies/Lightning Bugs

Learn how fireflies/lightning bugs glow

Background: Depending on where you live, you may call them fireflies or lightning bugs. These flashing beetles are found all over the United States and most of Canada, glittering in summer evening skies. They are easy to catch and do not bite people, making them perfect for kids to handle.

These insects light up through a process called bioluminescence. They produce a chemical called luciferin and mix it with enzymes and oxygen in their abdomen to create their pretty glow. They control how much air flows through their body and thus set the off-and-on pattern of their light. This ability is used to attract a mate and (possibly) to warn predators.

Activity: Catch some fireflies/lightning bugs in a jar and watch them closely. They are often in areas with tall grass and leaf litter near water, as they shelter there during the day. Draw one in your nature journal and include a second view showing its light-up abdomen.

- What does the light-producing abdomen look like? Does it remind you of anything?

- Do they get hot when they are flashing? (No. Heat is not generated when they light up.)

- What color is the light?

- About how long do they keep their light on? Do they flash while flying, while resting, or both?

Goldenrod Galls

Understand the life cycle of some flies, detect a parasitic relationship between a plant and an insect, see how a plant adapts to overcome stress

Background: Round swellings on the stems of goldenrod plants might look like seed pods, but they are actually the homes of a species of small insects. Gall flies insert an egg into the stem of the goldenrod plant in the spring. Within days, the larva hatches inside and feeds on the stem while being protected from the elements and predators. The plant grows around it, forming the gall. By the following spring, the fly has matured and it breaks out to mate. The female then lays eggs of its own in another stem, continuing the cycle.

Galls from other types of insects can be found on a variety of plants and trees as well. Look for them especially on oak leaves, appearing as small pods affixed to the surface.

Activity: Head out to a field to look for these balls on goldenrod stems.

- Examine the outside. Do you see any holes?

- If there is a hole, the gall fly could have matured and flown away. However, these galls are targets of overwintering birds like woodpeckers and black-capped chickadees. Does the hole look more like a fly exited the gall or that the gall was attacked from the outside?

- If there are no holes, the larva may still be inside. Carefully cut open the gall with a knife to see if you can find the tiny worm. Measure it and draw it in your nature journal. What does its home look like on the inside?

Raising Caterpillars

Witness the transformation of a caterpillar into a butterfly/moth firsthand, understand the life cycle of butterflies/moths, learn which food is eaten by a caterpillar, build a caterpillar habitat

One of the most exciting nature study experiences is raising caterpillars and releasing them as butterflies/moths. You can buy caterpillars and receive them in the mail, but it is more rewarding to find them in nature yourself. Some caterpillars eat only one kind of plant, while others eat a variety. The parent butterfly/moth lays eggs near the correct leaves so that the food source is available to the tiny caterpillars upon hatching.

To find your own to raise, look up common caterpillars in your area and note what they eat. Monarchs eat milkweed; black swallowtails eat Queen Anne's Lace, carrot leaves, dill, and others in that plant family, for example. Head outside and search for those plants, looking on the top and bottom of the leaves for eggs or caterpillars.

If you happen to come across a caterpillar while outside, identify it using a field guide, phone app, or an internet search. Be careful not to touch it until you know more about it, as some caterpillars are poisonous. Bring the caterpillar home, along with leaves from its host plant.

Caterpillar Habitat

Ready-made habitats are sold, but a two-liter bottle an inexpensive and easy-to-clean home for your caterpillar. Cut it a few inches/ centimeters from the bottom. Line the base with dry paper towels to catch the frass (droppings). Prop up sticks that reach toward the top of the bottle and supply leaves from the host plant. The plants will last longer if wrapped in wet paper towels, but don't leave standing water in the container, as the caterpillars could drown. Fit the top portion of the bottle into the bottom part. The caterpillar will be right at home.

INSECTS AND SPIDERS

The caterpillar will be hungry and needs a steady supply of food. The frass should be cleaned out every day or two. Pop off the top to maintain the habitat. Thankfully, the caterpillars are slow and don't have wings to escape yet.

Read about the metamorphosis of your caterpillar on the internet or in a field guide. This will help you know what to expect. These creatures go through the four phases of development like most insects: egg, larva (caterpillar), pupa (chrysalis or cocoon), and adult (butterfly or moth). As a larva/caterpillar, some go through very dramatic "instars" where they shed skin and look a bit differently in each stage.

As a pupa, a butterfly makes a chrysalis; a moth makes a cocoon. Some will emerge after a short time. Others will overwinter and come out in the spring, needing cold temperatures to finish their progress.

Newly emerged, the adult insect will need to dry its wings. It can be held as long as the wings are not touched. Instruct your child to place a finger underneath its feet. It will grab on tightly and want to be positioned with wings hanging downward, using gravity to dry straight. After a few hours, the wings will be stiff and the friend will fly away to mate.

Every time you notice a change in your caterpillar, document it in your nature journal. Create a dated log with a drawing and a written description of what happened.

Diagram a Butterfly

Get to know the anatomy of a butterfly

Catch a butterfly in a clear container or watch them visiting wildflowers. Draw a side view of the butterfly in your nature journal and label the parts: antenna, eye, proboscis (a straw that curls and extends for drinking plant nectar), head, thorax (middle body segment), abdomen (bottom body segment), legs, forewings (top wings), hindwings (bottom wings), and scales (on the wings). Notice which part of the body the legs and wings are attached to and that there are actually four wings that overlap to look like two.

Life Under Logs

Encounter insects and spiders living in the forest

Lift a log in the woods and identify the insects and spiders that you find beneath. Dig under the dirt and look closely in the crevices of the wood. Make a list of all those you find in your nature journal. Draw your favorite one. Count and write how many of each you saw.

- Did you find insects in groups or solo? Why?
- What makes this spot an ideal habitat for food and shelter?
- What did the creatures do when you lifted the log? Where did they go?
- Return the log to its resting place and wait a few minutes. Lift it again. Did the creatures return?

Flower Attraction

See the interdependence of insects and plants firsthand

Choose a single type of flower and make a list in your nature journal of all the insects attracted to it. Plants that heavily populate a wide area are good subjects, such as bluebells and sunflowers. Include illustrations of the plant and the insects you spot. Look for both flying and crawling bugs. Scan the stem and check the undersides of the leaves.

- What are the insects doing? Why are they attracted to the plants?
- How do some insects help the plant? (Pollination)
- How do some insects hurt the plant? (Eat their leaves, sucking plant sap from their leaves and stems)
- Did you see any spiders? Spiders, for the most part, do not eat plant nectar or leaves. Why are they there? (Feeding on the insects attracted to the plant)
- Can you explain how nature is working together?

"In every walk with nature, one receives far more than he seeks."

John Muir

Invertebrates

Invertebrates

Invertebrates are creatures that have no spines/backbones. The name comes from Latin: "In" means "without" and "vertebrate" is derived from the word for "joint" and has the concept of "turning." While a mammal has a spine that can twist and turn for movement, invertebrates have none. Some have an external shell that cannot bend, while others are completely soft.

This category includes creatures such as worms, snails, slugs, centipedes, millipedes, and a variety of seashore creatures like oysters, crabs, and starfish. Insects and spiders are also invertebrates, but they have been given a separate section in this book because of their great number.

Field Guides:

National Audubon Society Field Guide to Seashore Creatures

National Audubon Society Field Guide to Seashells

Books (Available free on archive.org):

A First Look at Animals Without Backbones by Millicent Selsam

Snails of Land and Sea by Hilda Simon

Discovery Dig

Find out who lives in soil, understand the difference between vertebrates and invertebrates, analyze specimens

Find an undisturbed patch of ground in the forest, a garden, or a field. Equip each person with a shovel, a pair of gloves, and a container for collecting creatures. Dig to find invertebrates living in the soil. Work carefully to avoid harming them. Analyze each creature you find to decide if it is an invertebrate. Instead of an internal backbone, invertebrates have a hard outer shell or are soft-bodied.

Draw and write about your findings in your nature journal. Then, set them free.

- How many invertebrates did you find? Which kinds?
- Do they live close together or solitarily?
- How did each kind behave when you captured them?

Earthworm Habitat

Learn about earthworms and their needs

Construct an earthworm habitat in a clear container. You could use a two-liter bottle with the top cut off, a large glass jar, or a bughouse. Pour in alternating layers of light sand and darker soil or compost. Wet each layer until damp but not soaked. Leave some room at the top to prevent the worms from escaping. Place leaves at the top to simulate nature.

You may find worms by digging in a garden or soft patch of ground, but purchase them from a bait shop if that fails. Set the worms in the habitat and cover the top with a piece of newspaper rubber-banded around the edge to keep the home dark and humid. Watch the worms for several days, spritzing water inside if it dries out. Comfortable worms will move about the soil freely; stressed worms will curl themselves into a tight bundle and stop moving.

Make notes in your nature journal about your observations.

If you keep your habitat long enough, you may also witness reproduction. Earthworms form a cocoon of eggs in the soil.

- When placed on top of the soil, what does a worm do? How fast does it burrow? How does it move?
- Look at the soil layers. How do earthworms move soil? How much soil do they move?
- Do the worms reuse tunnels or always make new ones?
- How do worms interact with each other?

Diagram a Worm

Get to know the anatomy of a worm

Dig up a worm or buy one from a bait shop. Draw it and diagram its parts in your nature journal: mouth, prostomium (tongue-like lobe just above the mouth), segments (ridges along the body), clitellum (flat part on the body, used for reproduction), and anus.

It can be hard to tell the difference between the mouth and the anus. Look for the clitellum. It is usually closer to the mouth. Note that they do not have eyes, ears, or noses. They sense light with the prostomium and feel the soil with their skin to navigate.

Diagram a Slug

Get to know the anatomy of a slug

Examine a slug and identify its parts: tentacles, eyes (on the tips of the tentacles), mantle (oval-shaped part on top of the head), pneumostome (breathing hole on the mantle), tail (part of the body from the mantle to the back tip), and foot (entire bottom section of the body that secretes mucus and expands and contracts to travel). Draw and label it in your nature journal.

Slug Watch

Encounter a slug or snail up close and watch its behavior

Background: Slugs and snails thrive in gardens, eating much of what they come across there: tender growing shoots, fleshy fruits and vegetables, live and decaying leaves, worms, insects, and even other slugs and snails. Since they depend on moisture, these well-watered habitats of soft soil and abundant leaves are perfect for them. They have places to hide during the drying heat of the day and an abundance of food to feast on at night.

While very similar, snails have a shell; slugs do not. Surprisingly, these common backyard creatures are part of the mollusk family, along with octopuses, squids, and clams.

Activity: Go outside after dark with a flashlight and look for slugs and snails in your garden beds. They hide during the day under mulch, stones, or soil. They emerge at night when the air is cool and moist. Look closely to see how their body works and watch what they do. Remember as much as you can and then draw and write about them in your nature journal when back inside.

- How do slugs move with only one "foot"? How fast are they? Can you spot the slimy track they leave?
- Can you see their eyes located at the ends of their tentacles?
- What does the mouth look like? How does it eat?
- What happens when you touch it?
- How do slugs and snails help the garden? How do they hurt it?

Millipede Watch

Encounter a millipede up close and observe its behavior

Background: These soil-dwelling creatures are named from the Latin for "thousand feet," though no varieties actually have that many. The effect of the numerous tiny legs, though, is fitting. Despite that number, these invertebrates are relatively slow-moving. They do not need speed to catch their primary diet of decaying plants. When threatened by toads, birds, or other predators, they spiral into a circle to protect their soft underbelly with their harder top shell. Centipedes are only distantly related and are quite different in structure and behavior.

Activity: Dig into moist soil to find millipedes. Gardens and forested land are common habitats, and they live in every state across the US. Millipedes do not bite and are safe to handle. Place the creature on top of a leaf and watch how it behaves. Look closely at its body. Use a magnifying glass. Draw what you see and write what you notice in your nature journal. Try counting the legs.

- Can you see the individual body segments? How many legs are on each part?

- What does the millipede do when it feels threatened? How does it protect itself?

- Compare several millipedes. Are they all the same size? Do they have the same number of legs? (Millipedes grow more body segments and legs as they mature.)

Ocean Walk

Examine ocean invertebrates, understand the difference between invertebrates and other sea creatures

Search an ocean beach for invertebrates. They may be more plentiful during low tide after a storm. Analyze each creature you see to see if it is an invertebrate- they are either soft or have a hard outer shell but not an internal backbone like a fish. Make a list in your nature journal with quick sketches of your finds. Use an app or field guide to identify them.

- How many invertebrates did you find? Which kinds?

- How are the invertebrates similar? Different?

- How did each kind get to the spot you found them?

Keep an Invertebrate Pet

Study an invertebrate over several days

Find an invertebrate and keep it as a pet for a few days. Mimic the environment you found it in.

For a snail, slug, or millipede: layer soil, fresh leaves, some moss, and a wet piece of decaying wood. Snails and slugs can easily climb container sides— secure the top with a rubber band around cheesecloth or screen.

For a freshwater or saltwater clam, carry it home in water from the source you found it along with enough sand for burrowing. Clams filter the water for food but can survive for 2-3 days with none. Return a short-term pet to the spot you found it in.

To keep a clam long-term, its habitat needs sufficient water and ample decaying matter. Some pet shops carry clams and supplies to sustain them, which might be an easier way to get started.

Spend time watching your new friend at eye level and track what it eats and how it behaves in your nature journal. Write up your experience and include illustrations.

"Let Nature be your teacher.

She has a world of ready wealth,

Our minds and hearts to bless—

Spontaneous wisdom breathed by health,

Truth breathed by cheerfulness."

William Wordsworth
"The Tables Turned"

Mammals

Mammals

People, dogs, squirrels, and cows are mammals, as well as some more unexpected animals like bats, platypuses, and whales. The characteristics that distinguish mammals from other animals in creation are that they have hair/fur, are warm-blooded, give birth to their offspring, and feed them with milk produced by the mother's mammary glands (from which "mammals" are named).

Field Guide:

National Audubon Society Field Guide to Mammals

Books (Available free on archive.org):

Big Tracks, Little Tracks by Millicent Selsam

Crinkleroot's Book of Animal Tracking by Jim Arnosky

Wild Tracks! : A Guide to Nature's Footprints by Jim Arnosky

Barnyard Family by Dorothy Childs Hogner

A First Look at Animals with Horns by Millicent Selsam

Animal Homes by Sally Cartwright

The Milk Makers by Gail Gibbons

How Kittens Grow by Millicent Selsam

Bats by Gail Gibbons

Beavers by Gail Gibbons

The How and Why Wonder Book of the Human Body by Martin Keen

Study 12

Closely observe 12 different kinds of mammals

Spend some time with a new mammal each week over a term/ semester. Start with your pets or those kept by a friend. Then, visit an animal shelter, zoo, or pet shop to encounter others. As you study each animal, note how it has the mammal characteristics: has hair/ fur, is warm-blooded, gives birth to offspring, and feeds babies with milk produced by the mother's mammary glands. As you interact with the mammal, consider how it interacts with you.

Draw the mammal and make notes about it in your nature journal. At the end of the term, review the similarities and differences between the mammals studied.

Bait Raccoons

Attract raccoons to see them up close

Background: Raccoons are nocturnal animals and are bold and crafty, notorious for sneaking around campgrounds to steal food outside the reach of the firelight. They eat almost anything, thriving in areas close to people where trash and cultivated gardens make easy and appetizing meals.

Activity: While camping or having a fire in your backyard, intentionally place treats on the perimeter and wait patiently for raccoons. Raw fruits and vegetables are healthy options. Listen and look for the glint of their reflective eyes in the dark. Shine a flashlight at the spot when you've "caught" one. Watch them quietly, then discuss what you noticed after they have scampered back out of view. Write about it in your nature journal.

- How do raccoons hold the food when they eat? What do they do with it while walking?

- How do you think the raccoon found the food you placed?

- Where did the raccoon go after it left?

MAMMALS

Deer Trails

Recognize trails made by deer, understand their behavior and habits

Background: Deer trails often cross hiking trails in forests. They are caused by the deer flattening vegetation as they repeatedly travel the same routes. These narrow paths usually go between a water source, a good feeding area, and a deer "bed" where they rest during the day.

Activity: Follow a deer trail to see where it goes.

Warning: Ticks may be present, though less active in winter. They wait on grass stems for deer and other mammals to pass. Wear repellant and check clothes and skin afterward.

- Did you find a water source? Feeding area? Deer resting spot? Draw a rough map of what you found in your nature journal.

- Deer rest during the day in hiding spots. Can you see any flattened areas in the grass? Why are they oval-shaped? (They match their body when lying down). Why did the deer choose this spot? (sheltered from the weather, has a good view of predators, enclosed for hiding.)

- Look for deer prints along the way. Measure and draw them to scale in your nature journal.

- Male deer shed their antlers and regrow new ones every year. You may be able to find them on the ground in late winter. However, rodents and other animals eat these antlers, so they are not around for long. If you do come across antlers, look at them closely. What color are they? What is the texture? Are they sharp or dull? Look at the spot they had connected to the deer's head- what do you notice? Sketch it on your page and write notes.

- In the spring/summer, male deer rub their antlers on trees to remove the velvet covering their new growth. They also rub their heads to mark their territory by leaving their scent. Can you find any abrasions on trees along the deer path? What do they look like? How can you tell if they are fresh or old?

Beaver Activity

Learn all you can about beavers from the clues they leave

Evidence of Beavers

Beavers are known as nature's architects. They chop down trees and transport them for building projects. They eat the bark and twigs while using the larger pieces to construct dams and build up their lodge. The dams raise the water level around the lodge to protect it from predators. Though they live near the water, they do not eat fish. A single family of beavers can significantly change a natural area.

Activity: Visit an area that has signs of beavers. Telltale evidence is small trees chopped down and chewed to a point. Draw and write about beavers in your nature journal.

If you encounter the beavers, they can be aggressive in defending their territory. Keep your distance and leave them alone. However, beavers are primarily nocturnal and rarely harm humans.

- What do trees look like after a beaver has chopped them down? Can you see teeth marks? How high off the ground do they cut it? Draw an example.

- What makes a tree a good target? Measure them with your hands. If you see some trees that have not been carried away, can you tell why?

- Do you see any trails they have worn along the ground? Where do the beavers seem to be coming from and going toward? Do you see prints? Draw one on your page.

- Look for the beaver lodge. They are built in the water and look like mounds of mud and branches. How must they get inside? (The doorway is located under the water, which protects them from predators.) Draw the hut and its surroundings in your journal. Write up what you notice about it.

- Can you spot any dams? How does it help protect the lodge? What is it made of?

Marine Mammals

Get to know marine mammals, encounter them in real life

Visit a zoo, aquarium, or marine animal sanctuary to study mammals that have ocean water habitats. Mammals such as seals, sea lions, otters, walruses, manatees, polar bears, and whales may be hard to spot in the wild and may not be native to your area. Draw and write about the marine mammals in your nature journal.

- While looking at the animal, consider how it meets the qualifications for being a mammal: Hair or fur (whiskers count!), warm-blooded, offspring are born alive and fed with milk produced by the mother's mammary glands.

- How is the mammal equipped for fishing? How does it move about in the water?

- Mammals are warm-blooded, regulating their own body temperature. How is this water mammal designed to keep warm? Cool?

Newborn Needs

Consider how newborn mammals interact with and depend on their mothers

Spend some time with a newborn mammal and its mother, such as a puppy, kitten, or farm animal. Use an online video if necessary. As you watch, discuss how this compares to human parents caring for their newborns. Draw the mother and the baby in your nature journal. Write about what you notice.

How were mammals designed to meet the needs of their young for:

- Food and drink? Warmth and comfort? Protection? Transportation?

Squirrel Watch

Notice the behavior of squirrels

Set out bread, corn, or seeds for squirrels to eat. As you watch, quietly say aloud everything you notice. Write about what you learn in your nature journal. Identify the squirrel in a field guide.

- In what ways are squirrels cautious? How are they brave?

- Watch how they move along the ground. Do they walk, hop, or do both?

- How are they able to climb trees? When they go up trees, are they facing head up or head down? When they go down, which way are they facing? What do their back feet look like? (Sharp claws and long fingers grasp the bark, back feet turn 180° when going down, which allows them to hang and steady their weight?

- While eating, how do they hold their food? Do they take large or small bites? How do they carry their food with them?

- Look closely at their fur and see what colors it has. Can you tell how thick their tail is under the bushy fur?

- How do they keep watch? Do they communicate with each other?

Human Body

Learn about some of the systems in the human body, locate body systems, draw conclusions

The human body has many different systems that serve specific purposes. List the following systems and name their function in your nature journal. Include a sketch for each.

The **skeleton** gives shape and strength to the body. Without it, we would be a puddle on the floor. Find and feel each individual bone from your fingertips to your shoulder. Look at someone's ribs and talk about the protection they give to the important organs behind them. Feel your face and head-bones. Feel the flexible cartilage in your nose and ears.

- Are all bones the same size and shape? What shapes did you feel? Why are they different?

- Why is the "rib cage" named as such? Cages, like at the zoo, keep things in and keep things out. Why do we need that for our bodies?

The **muscular** system enables our bodies to move. Think about what happens when we swallow, blink, and wiggle our toes. Find and feel the muscles that control each action.

- Flex your arm. How does your bicep muscle feel? Let your arm dangle. How does it feel now? Muscles move by contracting and relaxing. Can you feel the difference?

- Can bones move on their own? When you flex your arm, which bones move along with it?

Our **respiratory** system brings air in and out of the body. Feel what happens to your nose, throat, and lungs when you breathe in and out.

- Take a deep breath and feel your lungs fill with air. Do they remind you of anything else?

- Some body systems are voluntary, meaning we can choose to make them work, while others are involuntary, working without our conscious effort. Some are both. Is breathing voluntary or involuntary? Do we have to think about breathing? Can we choose to breathe?

- How often does our body need to breathe? Try holding your breath to find out.

The **cardiovascular** system distributes blood where it is needed, carrying oxygen and nutrients and transporting waste away. Trace veins in your wrists as far up your arms as possible. Listen to your pulse. This is the sound of the pump (the heart) powering this system.

- What do veins remind you of? (Maybe rivers, leaf veins, electrical system, or pipes)

- Are veins straight or curvy? Are they all the same width? Why do you think this is?

- When you get cut, what color is the blood? Is it always red? (Blood is always red- brighter when it has fresh oxygen, darker when not. Veins, however, look blue through the skin. As the outside light bounces off them, the color blue is most reflected. This is because it has the shortest wavelength, much like why blue is at the bottom of a rainbow.)

The **nervous** system transmits information from the senses to the brain and sends instructions from the brain to the muscles. Tap elbows and tickle toes to demonstrate this function.

- What do nerves remind you of? (A messenger or a phone conversation, maybe)

- Lightly touch the tip of a pencil to someone else's lips, then his/her back. Are nerves equally sensitive all over your body, or are some spots more receptive than others?

- Test your fingertips. Are they very sensitive or dull? Why are they designed that way?

ID Den Holes

Identify some common mammal dens/holes

Background: Some mammals live underground, a few create hideouts to duck into when danger is near, and others only head undercover to raise young. Winter is a wonderful time to look for these doorways, as they are more visible after the greenery has died back. As a bonus, snow or wet ground may capture tracks that can assist in identifying the creatures living there.

Activity: Visit a nature area and look for holes in the ground. Poke a stick into it to see how deep it is. See which direction the tunnel goes underground. To figure out who it belongs to, measure the hole. The inhabitants dig holes and passageways just large enough for themselves, keeping larger predators out.

In your nature journal, record the homes you identified. Draw the hole and write about the tell-tale signs. Include tracks spotted nearby.

Small holes (Less than 3 inches/8 centimeters)

A cleanly dug hole could be a chipmunk home. There are no clods of soil drawing attention to their homes. If you watch quietly and long enough, you are likely to see them scurrying nearby. They are very active during the day.

A small hole blocked by debris could be a mouse hole. Some Southwest mice even plug the opening of their holes with soil during the day for extra protection. If near dense grasses, sift through the stems to look for a matted highway system of well-trodden paths along the ground.

Several dime-sized holes dug near the roots of plants may be the home of a vole. Look also for signs of underground tunnels just below the soil surface.

A rectangular hole in the dry, sandy soil of the Western US is likely a kangaroo rat.

Holes with smooth edges and loose dirt in a fan shape coming from the hole could be the home of rats. Dirt is flung out during their digging and the hole edges are worn smooth by the comings and goings of the rats that live inside.

Large Holes (Greater than 3 inches/8 centimeters)

In the US West, numerous raised holes in an open area are probably prairie dogs. They live in populous colonies and are easy to spot popping in and out of their homes during the day.

Holes under buildings, porches, or other covered areas could be skunks. As another sign, they defecate in piles near their entrance.

Holes with a "soil porch" of flattened dirt could be made by woodchucks. Often, there are flies around the entrance.

A burrow with a mounded opening could belong to rabbits. Look for chewed vegetation nearby, as rabbits do not like to travel far from their home to feed.

Raised ridges weaving along the ground with a few piles of loose dirt are the feeding grounds of moles. You may not see actual holes, as moles rarely come to the surface.

Holes in the bank of a river or lake could be otter homes. They create multiple openings so they can access their den both underwater and from the land.

An area with several holes and disturbed ground could be badgers. They dig multiple holes for specific purposes, leaving piles of loose dirt. They live in the largest hole, with an opening measuring about 6-12 inches/15-30 centimeters. This is known as a sett. They leave their droppings in small holes nearby. They also dig to forage on small mammals hiding underground.

Some holes may be hard to identify. Raccoons, minks, and foxes take over the abandoned homes of others. Reptiles, spiders, and insects dig underground as well. Look for tracks to confirm. Snakes may go in and out of ground holes looking for prey, but most actually live above ground.

ID Prints

Identify some common mammal prints

Background: All mammals have feet and they leave their footprints as they walk through snow, sand, and wet mud. Canines leave prints with claw marks and their heel pad has two bumps. This includes dogs, foxes, coyotes, and wolves. Felines typically retract their claws while walking and their heel pad has three bumps. This includes house cats, bobcats, and lions. Bear prints are large and have five toes with claws, though the smallest toe may not mark. Deer have hooves with two divided toes. Squirrels have thin toes with small claws, four on their front paws and five on their back. Their tracks usually lead to a tree. Raccoon prints have five long fingers and more closely resemble a child's hands than animal paws.

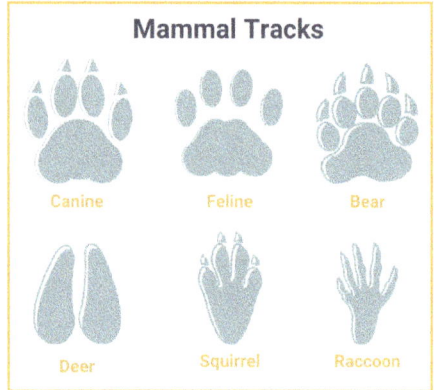

Mammal Tracks

Canine   Feline   Bear

Deer   Squirrel   Raccoon

Activity: Head outside to spot tracks and identify the travelers. Prints are especially visible on wet ground, such as near a water's edge, in snow, or after rain. Draw each print you find and label it in your nature journal. Measure the print dimensions and the stride between footfalls.

- Which prints are the hardest to identify? What can you look for to differentiate them?

- How can you tell the difference between the prints of a house cat and a lion? (Size, the likelihood of the animal in that location).

Feature Page

Differentiate between mammals and non-mammals, compare and contrast the physical features of mammals

Encounter mammals up close at a petting zoo and choose one kind of feature to compare. Title a page in your nature journal such as "Eyes of Mammals," "Mammal Fur," or "Mammal Footprints."

As you see each animal, first determine if it is a mammal. Review the qualifications of a mammal. They have hair/fur, are warm-blooded, give birth to their offspring, and feed them with milk produced by the mother's mammary glands. Rabbits, pigs, sheep, horses, goats are mammals. Chickens, ducks, and tortoises are not.

If it is a mammal, draw the chosen physical feature on your nature journal page. Write notes if needed.

- Did all mammals have this feature?
- How were the features similar? (Size, shape, color)
- How were the features different? (Size, shape, color)
- Do you have this feature? How is yours different than these animals?

"While all that borrows life from Thee is ever in Thy care;

And everywhere that we can be, Thou, God, art present there."

Issac Watts
"I Sing the Mighty Power of God"

Reptiles

Reptiles

Lizards, turtles, alligators, and snakes are examples of reptiles. Members of this group have vertebrae and are covered with scales. Most reproduce by laying eggs. They are all cold-blooded; they control their body temperature by using their surroundings. On cool days, look for reptiles warming themselves on rocks. When the weather is hot, check the shade. If you live in a climate where you are not likely to encounter reptiles in the wild, see them up close at a nature center, zoo, or pet shop.

Field Guide:

National Audubon Society Field Guide to Reptiles and Amphibians

Books (Available free on archive.org):

The How and Why Wonder Book of Reptiles and Amphibians by Robert Mathewson

Slither and Crawl : Eye to Eye with Reptiles by Jim Arnosky

A First Look at Snakes, Lizards, and Other Reptiles by Millicent Selsam

A First Look at Poisonous Snakes by Millicent Selsam

Alligators and Crocodiles by Herbert Zim

Study 12

Learn about 12 different kinds of reptiles

Pick a different reptile to study in person each week over the term/semester. As you observe the animal, consider each of the characteristics of reptiles: has a backbone, is covered with scales, lays eggs, and is cold-blooded. Draw your specimen in your nature journal and write your observations about it. Count and record anything that can be numbered. Include alternate views and close-ups when helpful.

Turtle Watch

Practice watching patiently and quietly, notice everything you can

Encounter a turtle at a nature center, zoo, or in the wild. Their natural habitat is in or around water, such as ponds, lakes, rivers, and the ocean. Watch the turtle without interfering with it. Say aloud what you notice about its appearance and its behavior. Draw it and write about it in your journal.

- Where was the turtle? Why was it there?
- What was it doing? Based on what you saw, how active do turtles seem in general?
- How did it move? Does its shell drag when it walks, or does it lift it up? How fast can it walk?

Turtle Equipment

See how turtles are equipped for living in their environments

Go to a nature center, zoo, or pet shop where you can see both a water-based and a land-based turtle. Notice as much as you can about a turtle that lives primarily in the water, such as a red ear slider or a sideneck. Look at the shape and texture of the shell, the design of its feet, its beak (mouth), etc. Draw this in your nature journal, writing notes that explain how its features help it thrive in water. Next, consider the appearance of a land-based turtle, such as a box turtle. Draw it in your nature journal and write about how it is designed to live on land.

- What traits do all turtles have? What is unique to water turtles What is special in the design of land turtles?

Diagram a Turtle

Get to know the anatomy of a turtle

Spend some time with a turtle, either observed in the wild or encaged at a nature center, zoo, or pet shop.

REPTILES

Find each of these parts: eye, beak (mouth), neck, legs, nails, carapace (top shell), plastron (bottom shell), scutes (plates on the shell), and tail. Draw and label each part in your nature journal.

Safe Snakes, Dangerous Snakes

Recognize local snakes, understand what makes some snakes dangerous to humans

Background: Snakes eat small animals like mice and toads, usually alive. Some swallow the animal whole, while others squeeze their prey first. These types are relatively safe for people. Their preference is to slither away to safety. If they are surprised and bite, the wound is usually not serious.

However, there are dangerous snakes and they must be avoided. When they bite their prey or a perceived threat, they inject a poison called "venom," which is toxic.

Activity: Learn which snakes live in your area through online research. Become familiar with what they look like and where you are likely to find them.

In your nature journal, make a list of "safe" snakes, which are those that contain no venom. Make a second list of venomous, dangerous snakes. Illustrate this list to help in committing them to memory. As you hike, be on the lookout for these safe snakes and, especially, the dangerous ones. This project could span several weeks.

- Do the "safe" snakes have similar traits as each other?
- Do the "dangerous" snakes have anything visibly in common?
- Where are you most likely to encounter venomous snakes in your area?
- What should you do if you see a venomous snake outside?
- If you encounter a snake and are not sure if it is safe or dangerous, what should you do?

Snake Patterns

Become familiar with snakeskin designs

Visit a nature center, zoo, or pet shop to see the variety of patterns on snake skins. Each type of snake has a specific design. This is the primary way to identify them.

Draw equal squares in your nature journal and draw or paint the pattern of each snake in its own box. Label each swatch with the snake's type.

Snake Patterns

- Do all the snakes you watched have their patterns repeating in some way?

- What are the most common colors for the snakes in your sample? How do those shades help camouflage them in their environment?

- Look closely. Is each scale a single color or multiple colors? What shape are the scales? Are they all the same on the same snake? Do all snakes have the same shape scales?

Snake Watch

Observe a snake, practice watching patiently and quietly, observe everything you can

Observe a snake found at a nature center, zoo, or in the wild. Their natural habitat includes forests, grassy meadows, water bodies, deserts, and swamps.

Say aloud everything you notice about its appearance and its behavior. Identify the snake and make a nature journal entry with what you observed.

- Where was the snake? Why was it there? What was it doing?

- What is its skin like? Does it remind you of anything?

- Snakes have no legs and feet. How can they move? How fast do they go?

Catch a Lizard

Encounter a lizard up close, learn about a lizard's behavior and habitat

Background: Lizards live in most climates, but they can be hard to encounter. They have many predators. They are always on the lookout and hide whenever they feel threatened. They may dwell on the ground or in trees. Some species live in dense forests, while others prefer the desert conditions of the southwest.

They are all cold-blooded and need the heat of the sun to stay active. When temperatures dip, they move slowly or not at all, conserving their energy. Lizards, therefore, are most active during the warmth of the day. You may find them basking on warm rocks or lying in wait for passing insects to eat.

Activity: Search the internet to identify lizards that live in your area. Discover which environment you are most likely to see them and then go exploring to try to catch one. Choose a cooler day; they are slower at lower temperatures. If you cannot find and catch a lizard in the wild, see them up close at a nature center, zoo, or pet shop.

Create a nature journal entry of your experience.

- Which lizards are native to your area?
- Where did you find the lizard?
- What is it doing?
- Look closely at its skin. How is it similar/different from other reptiles you have encountered?
- How does the lizard move? Is it slow or quick? Does it seem affected by the temperature?

Rocks, Minerals, Soil

Rocks, Minerals, Soil

Minerals are naturally occurring solids such as halite (salt), graphite (pencil lead), quartz, and copper. They are neither living nor derived from plants or animals. In general terms, they are a pure, consistent material. In technical terms, they have a definite chemical composition and ordered atomic arrangement.

Rocks, on the other hand, are made up of one or more kinds of minerals that have gone through a process to join them together. If you look closely at a rock, you may see speckles of colors and textures, yet the rock is solid. These processes include, "igneous" (formed by cooled magma), "sedimentary" (layers of material settling and compressing), and "metamorphic" (igneous or sedimentary rocks changed by temperature, pressure, or force).

Soil is the top of the Earth's crust, made up of minerals and rocks along with organic matter, water, air, and living organisms. Soil is essential for growing plants and also serves as a habitat for some insects and animals. Soil types are classified by how much sand, silt, and clay they contain.

Field Guides:

National Audubon Society Field Guide to Rocks and Minerals

National Audubon Society Field Guide to Fossils

Books (Available free on archive.org):

The How and Why Wonder Book of Rocks and Minerals by Nelson Hyler

Birth of an Island by Millicent Selsam

A First Look at Rocks by Millicent Selsam

Caves and Caverns by Gail Gibbons

Rock Analysis

Carefully examine rocks, understand the variety of colors, shapes, and textures

Collect interesting rocks from a riverbank, mountain trail, or beach. Illustrate them in your nature journal, noting the flecks, lines, and colors you see. A magnifying glass or travel microscope may be helpful to see the tiniest details.

- Look at each rock. Is it a solid color or is it made up of several colors? Which colors do you see? Are there flecks or lines? Does it sparkle? What is the texture? Are the edges round or sharp?

- Are any of your rocks similar to each other? How so?

- Looking at your collection, are rocks all the same? Why do you think they are different?

Hammer

Experiment with how rocks break under force, use information to predict outcomes

Brainstorm natural forces that wear down and crack rocks into smaller pieces. For example, rivers both crash rocks into each other and slowly wear them down into smaller pieces over time. Rain carries mild acids from the atmosphere and erodes some types of minerals. Earthquakes and landslides crumble rocks with great force. Water trickles into small crevices and pries them open as it freezes. Plant roots can invade cracks and separate rocks as they grow. People and animals grind rocks under their feet.

Experiment with how rocks break apart under force. Collect a variety of rocks and give each child a hammer. You will need a hard surface like a larger rock or concrete to hammer against. As you hit the rocks, note what happens to them. Write about and illustrate what discover in your nature journal.

- How does each rock break apart: turn to powder? break into sharp sections? split along smooth lines?

- Now that you have experimented, can you tell beforehand how each rock will behave when struck? What are some clues?

- Which rocks are easiest to break apart? Which rocks require a harder hit? Can you tell by looking or feeling?

Collect and Classify

Practice organizing and sorting by characteristics, discern rock formation types

Collect rocks while hiking. Once you have several specimens, decide as a group how to classify them. You may choose to do it by color, appearance, hardness, texture, shape, etc. Place them in like piles.

Explain that scientists usually categorize rocks by how they were formed. Sedimentary rocks were created as layers of minerals or organic matter settled and were compressed over time. They are the easiest to identify because they have defined stripes made up of small grains. Igneous rocks were made by cooled magma. That process caused crystals to form. Metamorphic rocks are either sedimentary or igneous rocks that have been altered by a force. They have layers or crystals in wavy swirls.

Look for examples of each type from your collection and rearrange them into these groups. Draw one example of each type in your nature journal (if you were able to find all three), and write about the defining characteristics.

- What do all of your rocks have in common? What are some differences?

- Which type of rock (igneous, sedimentary, or metamorphic) is your favorite? Why?

- If a friend showed you a rock, how could you help him/her identify how it was formed?

Fossils

Simulate how fossils are formed, discover the information fossils preserve and what is lost

Background: Many things in nature die and decompose over time. Soft tissues decompose quickly, but even harder ones like bones and shells are broken down and are washed away over long periods of time. Often, other members of creation use the materials and no trace is left. Dead animals are eaten by other animals. Plant material breaks down and is incorporated unrecognizably into the soil.

However, if conditions are just right, evidence of the item is preserved in the form of a fossil. The item makes an imprint in the rock or sediment where it has fallen. The fossil could be a hollow shell where the item had once been, known as a "mold fossil." If minerals seep into that hollow opening and harden to fill the space, a "cast fossil" is formed. The third type of fossil is where the actual item has been petrified, known as a "true form fossil."

Activity: Demonstrate how mold fossils are formed by pressing nature finds in clay. Small, hard items work best for this experiment, such as acorns or seashells. Allow the children to sandwich the item between a bigger piece of clay. Remove the item to see the imprint.

If with a group, have each child make a mold fossil secretly and then have their friends guess the item using only the clues left by the imprint. Show the item afterward.

Write about fossils in your nature journal.

- What information is preserved in a fossil? (Shape, texture, size, structure)
- What information about the item is lost? (Color, scent, internal makeup, behavior)

Mud Shakes

Conduct an experiment to learn about the makeup of soil, see the difference between soils from different locations

Background: Soil is primarily a combination of sand, silt, and clay. The ideal garden soil is 40% sand, 40% silt, and 20% clay. This is known as "loam." Soil with a high percentage of sand can drain too well, not holding nutrients and water for plant roots. Soil with a lot of clay can be too heavy for roots to grow in, and it can become soggy with water that does not drain fast enough. Loam is a perfect balance. To measure soil composition, you can mix a shovelful in a jar of water and let it settle.

Activity: In this experiment, sample different soils to see what they are made of. Bring quart-size (or larger) jars filled halfway with water and sealed with a lid. You will need one jar for each soil sample you plan to take. Have a hand trowel and labeling materials: masking tape and a pen.

Sample the soil from several spots: your garden, the forest floor, a field, the riverbank, a nature trail, etc. Label each jar with the location and shovel in enough soil to bring the water level near the top. You could allow each student to choose a location and take a sample.

Shake each jar to mix everything thoroughly and then leave it to settle. After a few minutes, you will see the distinct layers: sand at the bottom, silt in the middle, and clay at the top. Organic matter floats on the surface. If there is a lot of clay, the water may not be completely clear for a day or two, but you should have a general idea after several minutes.

Sand has the largest, heaviest particles and therefore falls to the bottom first. By looking closely, you can see individual grains. Silt has medium-sized particles and forms a layer right above the sand. It looks silky. Clay is made up of the smallest particles and takes the longest to fall, keeping the water cloudy until it fully settles as a top layer. Clay may be red, brown, or grey. Anything floating on the water surface is organic matter from dead plants and animals.

All three of the sand/silt/clay layers may be present, just two or (rarely) just one. Compare and discuss the differences in the soils from your locations. You could estimate the percentages and figure out the classification using an online soil chart.

Write up your findings in your nature journal, drawing the jars and the layers for each sample location.

Soil Samples

Location:
Description:

- Which sample had the most sand? Silt? Clay? Based on where you found them, why do you think that was the case?

- Compare the differences in color between each sample. What makes them that way?

- Why does the sand sink to the bottom first? Why is silt next and clay last? Can you see the difference in particle sizes?

- How did the water help sort the soil components that were previously all mixed together in the ground?

Natural Compost

See firsthand how wood breaks down and nourishes soil in the wild

Background: After plants die, they decompose. Invertebrates and fungi live on the plant material, breaking it down and recycling it into a nutrient-rich soil component called compost.

Activity: Find a decaying log in the forest to investigate how nature composts. Before touching it, notice everything you can about the log.

- How can you tell it is decaying? Why is it doing so?

- What would happen in our world if nothing decayed?

Next, roll the log over and look beneath.

- What is the texture of the soil? Are there pieces of wood in it? How are these different than the wood of the log?

131

- Scrape away the soil, layer after layer, to see how it is affected by the composting log. Does the color or texture change as you go deeper?

- Compare the soil under the log to soil on open ground nearby. How are they the same? How are they different?

Write up your findings about natural composting in your nature journal. Illustrate the log and the soil as you explain the process in writing.

Examine Sand

See how sand is made up, use a microscope or magnifying glass to observe tiny details, understand how sand is formed and how it looks different depending on its environment

Background: Sand comes from the surrounding environment. Predominately, white sand is either made of quartz from parent rocks that were eroded by water or the undigested coral from parrotfish. Black sand is often made of tiny pieces of volcanic rock. Brown sands are likewise made of broken-up local rocks and shells of marine creatures.

Activity: Collect sand from a creek, river, lake, or ocean beach. Look at the sample under a microscope or magnifying glass. Explain what you see. Draw and describe each particle in your nature journal. Likely, your sample will have a mix of colors and sources. The water body may have broken down nearby materials or washed up sediment carried from a long distance.

- What colors do you see?

- What shapes are there?

- How many different particles can you count?

- What do the grains of sand remind you of?

- Are there any large rocks or cliffs of the same color nearby?

Stars & Sky

Stars and Sky

To untrained eyes, stars appear to be randomly scattered across the night sky. However, they are deliberately set and entirely consistent, reliable enough for the ship captains of past days to navigate by. The stars always stay in the same position in relationship to each other. Our view of them shifts as we orbit around our sun, such that the Big Dipper is the same size and shape, but its distance from the horizon changes. Some constellations slip out of our view, visible in the summer, but not in the winter, for example.

The arrangement of the stars has been grouped into recognizable shapes (constellations) by people throughout history. Myths and stories have been crafted about them. A book like "Find the Constellations" by HA Rey presents these together for a fascinating study. Combine a study of star charts with trips to see the night sky for yourself.

The moon changes its appearance to us a little bit every day, and it can be seen traveling across the sky in a single evening. It is made up of rock and metal like the Earth and does not have a light of its own. The moon reflects light from the sun and is always half-lit. The part facing the sun reflects its light, while the opposite side is in the dark of its own shadow.

However, the illuminated portion we see depends on our view from Earth. During a "full moon" (fully lit), we can see the whole round face. During a "new moon" (fully dark), we can only see the shadowed side. Between these extremes, the moon grows in appearance ("waxes") from a sliver to a full moon, then "wanes," seemingly shrinking back to a dark new moon. Our word "month" comes from the moon as this full cycle takes about that portion of time.

While the sun always rises in the morning and sets in the evening, the moon is visible at different times. Our view of the moon is dependent on the positions of the Earth, moon, and sun. Surprisingly, over a month's time, the moon accompanies us as much by day as it does by night. It is only at the full moon that it rises in the East just as the sun sets in the West. We only associate the moon with night because it is easier for us to see then. An online chart can show you the "moonrise" and "moonset" times for each day.

Field Guide:

National Audubon Society Field Guide to the Night Sky

Books (Available free on archive.org):

Find the Constellations by H.A. Rey

The Planets by Gail Gibbons

Stargazers by Gail Gibbons

The Moon Book by Gail Gibbons

Shooting Stars by Herbert Zim

Study 12

Be able to recognize 12 different constellations in the sky

Background: Constellations do not actually exist. They are imaginary shapes people have made up while looking at the arrangement of the stars in the sky. They have drawn imaginary lines between them to envision pictures of animals, warriors, and symbols. The stars always stay in the same formation but change location in the sky throughout the year. Sailors used constellations to tell direction and farmers looked at the sky to determine dates.

Activity: Using a book or a website, pick a new constellation to learn each week over the term/semester. Draw the star arrangement in your nature journal, labeling it with the name. Watercolor a swath of dark paint or mount a rectangle of black paper in your journal and use a white gel pen for the stars. Use bigger dots for brighter stars or use specific symbols. Star brightness is rated by six magnitudes. A book on constellations may detail these. If there is a related story to the constellation, you could retell it in your journal as well.

Find your constellation in the night sky. Drive to a spot away from city lights to have the best view. Because of the Earth's orbit around the sun, some constellations may not be visible at all times of the year, but a good resource should tell you when to expect them.

It can be much more difficult to spot constellations in the actual sky compared to looking at them on star charts. There are several apps that can help you out if you are stuck. You simply point your phone to the sky and it will identify them for you. However, have your kids give it a good try before consulting or confirming with an app. You can use a high-powered flashlight to trace the constellations in the sky if your kids need help spotting them.

Planetarium Show

Meet an astronomy expert, learn about space

Background: Planetariums are theaters with domed ceilings that simulate outer space. Shows are designed to teach about stars, space travel, the sun, and the Earth, giving an immersive learning experience to people who may never be able to leave the planet.

Activity: Attend a program at a planetarium to learn about the night sky. A knowledgeable instructor can show you so much more than you can see from the ground. Encourage your kids to ask the instructor at least one question after the show.

Write about the experience in your nature journal. Illustrate and describe what you learned.

Visit an Astronomy Club

Experience night sky events with local astronomy enthusiasts

Look for a hobby astronomy club that meets locally. Often these will host public events based on current astronomical events to educate people about the night sky. They may have high-powered telescopes available to look through as well as "experts" who can tell you what to look for. If they do not have public events, perhaps they would welcome you to come for a field trip. The enthusiasm of these hobbyists is contagious.

Moon Phase Log

Understand that the moon reflects the sun and does not produce light on its own, see how the moon's appearance changes throughout its cycle, collect data and create a chart, analyze patterns

Background: The moon does not have any light of its own, but appears bright because it reflects the sun. Like the Earth, the moon is a sphere and always has one side lit while the other is dark. The side closest to the sun is illuminated while its other half is in its own shadow.

Moon Reflects the Sun

Moon Phases
Viewed from Earth

Waning

New

Waxing

Moon's Orbit

However, from Earth, the moon seems to change shape, appearing as a crescent, half of a pie, a lopsided circle, or a full disk. This variance is due to the angle from which we are viewing the moon. As it orbits the Earth one full time per month, that angle changes slightly along with the amount of "lit" moon surface we see.

At the new moon, we see only the dark side of the moon. In the following days, we see a little more of the lit surface starting from a small sliver and growing. This is called "waxing." At the full moon, we can see the whole lit side perfectly. From then on, we see a little less of that lit side ("waning") until it disappears altogether at the next new moon.

Activity: Keeping a log of the "shape" of the moon will help you see the pattern and progression for a complete lunar cycle. In your nature journal, paste a single-month calendar page, draft one, or get moon phase printable from naturestudycollective.com. You may choose to start the study on the first day of the month or from the new moon. Each day/night, look at the moon and draw what you see. Consult a moonrise and moonset website for viewing times. When cloudy skies block the moon, you can leave that spot blank in your chart and later estimate what you would have seen using the pattern of the data.

- Does the moon come out at the same time each day? (While we might think of the moon coming out for the night as the sun sets, it follows its own schedule, which the students should notice as they do this activity. Some days in each month, it only appears during the daylight hours when it is more difficult for us to see.)

- How long is the lunar cycle, from new moon to new moon? (29.53 days, about one month. The word "month" is derived from the word "moon.")

- Can you explain in your own words why the moon phases exist?

Sunrise/Sunset Watch

Observe the changes to sunlight when it nears the Earth's horizon

Background: Sunlight looks white to our eyes but is actually made up of a spectrum of colors. When scattered by a prism or water droplets, we see the full rainbow of ROYGBIV (red, orange, yellow, green, blue, indigo, and violet). Rainbows are a treat when conditions are just right. However, something very similar happens every day as the sun rises and sets. As the sunlight is near the horizon, it is spread out as it travels sideways through our atmosphere. If clouds do not block the view, we can see the array of colors. Some colors may be missing from the ROYGBIV spectrum, but those visible will always be in order.

Activity: Watch the sun rise or set and record what it looks like every 15 minutes. Divide your nature journal page into long rectangles and record the colors, clouds, and brightness you see. Include what the sky looks like when the sun is fully below the horizon.

- What colors do you see? How is this similar to a rainbow?

- When the sun is on the horizon, are the colors more or less vivid? Can you feel a temperature change? Why?

Sundial

Learn how the Earth turns in relation to the sun, use a sundial to tell time

Background: Though the sun looks as if it climbs our sky from the East in the morning and travels West until it dips below our horizon in the evening, the sun is not actually moving. It is the Earth that rolls around on its axis, changing our view of the stationary sun.

Activity: Imagining these movements of the Earth in our surroundings is a very different perspective compared to seeing the diagrams on the pages of a book.

- Point to the East, where the sun seems to rise, and to the West where it seems to set. Which way is the Earth spinning? (We are rotating toward the East.)

- What happens at sunset? (The Earth is turning away from the sun and the sun is moving out of view over our horizon.)

The sun's path is so constant and predictable that we can tell time by it, using a sundial. Look for one posted at a nature center, local park, garden, school, or community building. While decorative, these are scientific instruments that can be very accurate if set up correctly. On a sunny day, the center pin will cast a shadow accurately on the time inscribed along the perimeter, much like the hands of a clock.

- What time does the sundial say right now? How does this compare to the actual time, as read on a digital clock? If it is wildly off, the sundial was installed incorrectly.

- How is it possible that a simple sundial like this can tell time? How predictable is the sun?

- How must the sundial be oriented? If it were turned, even slightly, would it be correct?

Draw the sundial and describe how it works in your nature journal.

NASA.gov

Learn about outer space and space technology

Background: NASA is part of the US government with the mission to study the universe. To accomplish this, they conduct scientific research through exploration, while developing the necessary technology along the way.

Activity: Visit the NASA website to learn about current space missions and space technology. There are live videos of launches and landings and current events at the International Space Station. Choose one event to learn about and watch as they live-stream the mission. Write about it in your nature journal, including the date, the goal, the people involved, the vehicles used, and the result.

Shooting Stars Watch

Witness "shooting stars" in person, learn about meteors and our atmosphere

Background: Shooting stars are actually not stars at all, but space rocks that burn up as they enter our Earth's atmosphere. "Comets" are larger clumps of ice and dust. "Asteroids" are large space rocks, while "meteoroids" are small space rocks. If they enter Earth's atmosphere, they start burning up and are now called "meteors." If any part lands on the Earth (which is rare), it is labeled a "meteorite." We can predict when meteor showers happen as we monitor space and see groups of meteoroids traveling toward us. Also, individual meteors occur from time to time.

Activity: Find out when a meteor shower will be visible in your area and go on a nighttime adventure to see it. A website like almanac.com lists dates and viewing times.

The conditions have to be suitable for the best show. The weather has to be clear. Meteors may be shooting across the sky, but clouds will block your view. You need a dark, open sky. Drive out to a rural spot away from city lights. Though night seems dark to us everywhere, cities emanate a glow that can make light coming from the universe hard or impossible to see. Ideally, there will be no tall trees or buildings to block parts of the sky.

It may take some time for your eyes to adjust to the dark. Use a red flashlight to get around, as this will not affect your night vision. Lie flat on your backs on blankets and be patient. Call out when you see meteors. Back at home, do a nature journal entry about what you saw.

- Why do you think some "shooting stars" are short and others are long? (Size of the meteor, what it is made up of, speed it is traveling, angle it enters our atmosphere)

- How is Earth's atmosphere designed to protects us from these space rocks?

- What would happen if they all hit our Earth without shrinking and slowing?

"Nature-study cultivates in the child a love of the beautiful ... a perception of color, form and music ... But more than all, nature-study gives the child a sense of companionship with life out-of-doors and an abiding love of nature."

Anna Botsford Comstock
"Handbook of Nature Study"

Trees
& Shrubs

Trees and Shrubs

A tree is simply a really tall plant. It has roots, a stem, leaves, and it makes food using photosynthesis. Unlike most plants, they can live hundreds of years and grow much taller and stronger.

Shrubs are similar to trees though shorter and often have multiple stems instead of a single trunk. However, there is no official categorization. Some differentiate by height: anything short is a shrub, and anything tall is a tree. Some species of trees can be trimmed and then be considered shrubs. Some shrubs can be cared for to encourage height, growing into a tree.

There is overlap, but in general, trees and shrubs are either "deciduous," growing broad leaves in the spring and losing them in the fall, or "evergreen," growing needles that stay all year long.

Field Guides:

National Audubon Society Field Guide to Trees: Eastern Edition

National Audubon Society Field Guide to Trees: Western Edition

www.arborday.org/trees/whattree/

Books (Available free on archive.org):

Tell Me, Tree: All About Trees for Kids by Gail Gibbons

Thanks to Trees: The Story of Their Use and Conservation by Irma Webber

Crinkleroot's Guide to Knowing the Trees by Jim Arnosky

A First Look at Leaves by Millicent Selsam

Maple Tree by Millicent Selsam

Study 12

Get to know 12 different kinds of trees or shrubs that grow locally

Study one tree or shrub per week over the term/semester, starting with those in your yard or neighborhood. For each tree/shrub, identify its name and learn about it in a field guide.

In your nature journal, sketch the general shape and trace/paint a single leaf. Mount a physical leaf on the opposite page, sealing it with packing tape to preserve it. Completing this project will result in knowing a good variety of trees and shrubs that you will continue to encounter throughout your life.

- Do you see any fruits, flowers, or seeds? Draw them in your journal.
- Compare the height of the tree. Is it taller than you? Taller than a house?
- Measure the width of the trunk. Can you wrap your fingers around it? Can you encircle it with your arms?
- Is this tree similar to another tree you have studied? How so?

ID the Neighborhood

Know the trees that live around you, practice drawing maps

Walk around your yard or neighborhood and draft a rough map of the trees that live near you. Choose a symbol for your house, the road, and the trees. Identify the tree names using a field guide and label them on your map.

- Look at how the trees are arranged. Do you think someone planted them that way or did they grow there naturally?
- What is the most common kind of tree in your area? Why do people like this kind?

Diagram a Tree

Get to know the anatomy of a tree

Draw the general shape of a tree and label the parts in your nature journal: root, trunk, crown (general top section of branches with leaves), branch, spray (branch tips), and leaf. Accurately represent the proportions of the crown's height compared to the trunk. Consider if your tree is wider than it is tall or the other way around.

Bloom Tree Buds

Witness how leaves emerge from their buds

In late winter or early spring, cut off a twig from a tree or shrub that has unopened buds. Bring it home and place it in water, keeping it in a spot where you can watch it throughout the day. Draw it on a left side page in your nature journal, showing the arrangement of the buds on the wood as well as the precise color and texture of the closed capsule. Date the page.

In time, the flowers or leaves will unfurl from their protected packages. On the facing page, draw the bloomed twig with as much detail as you can.

- How long did it take for the flowers or leaves to emerge?
- What happened to the scales that had been protecting the buds?
- What color and shape are the new flowers or leaves?
- Which buds opened first, those toward the bottom or the tip? The buds on the main branch or the side branches?
- Did any buds not open at all?

Adopt a Tree

Become familiar with the seasonal changes of trees

Background: Deciduous trees go through radical transformations as they make the most out of the seasons. They sprout all new leaves in the spring. They create food, growth, and seeds throughout the warm, sunny summer. Cool autumn days trigger the tree to conserve its energies in its roots while the leaves dry up and fall off. It waits through the winter for spring to return.

Activity: Choose a deciduous (non-evergreen) tree to "adopt" for the year, either from your yard or a place you frequently visit. A maple or a fruiting variety will have dramatic changes that are especially interesting to study. Visit your tree in the fall, winter, spring, and summer, creating a nature journal entry with what you notice. You may want to divide a single sheet into four sections, filling one part for each season, or give each season a full page on consecutive sheets. Note what the leaves look like, the overall shape, and the presence of fruits or seeds. (This activity is based on Charlotte Mason's "The Study of Trees," described in "Home Education" on pages 53-54.)

Fall

- How does your tree prepare for the winter?
- Do its leaves change color? Which colors? Which leaves change first?
- Do green leaves, changing leaves, and brown leaves feel the same?

Winter

- What is the overall shape of your tree?
- Look closely at the twigs. Can you see leaf scars from where the leaves were attached before they fell? What shape are these? Compare to another type of tree nearby. Are they the same or different?

TREES AND SHRUBS

- What do the leaf buds look like? Where are they on the tree? How is it protected? Are they arranged mirror-image on the twig like hops, or do they alternate like footsteps?
- Can you spot any animals using the tree for shelter during the winter? How do they use it?

Spring

- How do the leaf buds unfurl?
- What color are they when they emerge? Are older leaves the same color and shade?
- Which leaves open first: Those closer to the ground or toward the top? From the middle or the edges? Is it random?
- Does your tree have any flowers (even if they do not look like typical flowers)?

Summer

- What kind of fruit and seeds does your tree produce?
- Are these seeds protected in any way? Can you open one with your fingers?
- What color are summer leaves? Are any exactly the same size and shape?
- Can you see any birds or animals that feed on the seeds?

Classify

Understand the basic tree and leaf shapes

Look at a tree from a distance and classify its overall crown shape. The crown is the top section of the tree, from the lowest branches to the highest tip. Is it conical, columnar, vase, broad, pyramidal, weeping, round, open, or irregular? If it has been pruned and intentionally shaped by landscapers, see if you can tell what its natural outline would be. Do a quick sketch in your nature journal, capturing the overall silhouette without necessarily representing every branch.

Get up close and consider a single leaf. Is the leaf smooth with a flat contoured edge, toothed with a jagged profile, or lobed with defined sections? Next, is it a simple leaf- a single leaf connected to a twig on the tree? Or, is it compound with many leaves attached to a central stem? If the leaf is compound, are the leaves arranged on the stem alternately taking turns, oppositely mirroring each other, or whorled in bunches? Draw or trace the leaf in your nature journal and record the shape names.

As an added challenge, try to spot an example for each category of crown and/or leaf shapes as you hike.

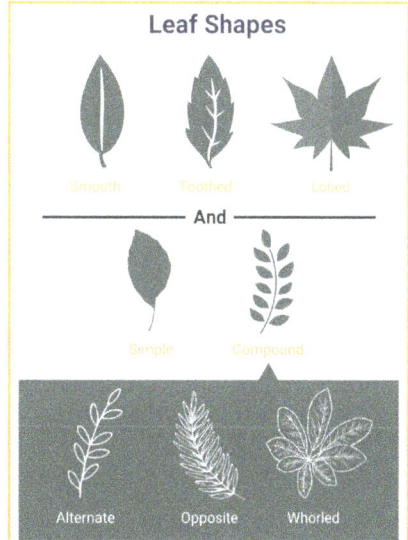

Tree History

Understand how trees grow, learn how to read tree rings to know a tree's history

Background: Each year, trees grow slightly. They get taller by adding to the splayed tips of each twig, they dig deeper by shooting down lengthening roots, and they grow wider by adding a layer to everything: trunk, branches, twigs, and roots. This layer shows up as a visible ring. Vigorous growth in the spring produces a wider, light-colored ring. Slower summer growth adds a thin dark ring.

By looking at this ring pair, we can learn a lot about the history of that tree. During years of favorable conditions, the tree grows more by adding thicker rings. Stressors like drought, pests, or competition limit the tree to producing thinner rings. If the rings are lopsided, it could be that something was pushing against them, causing asymmetric growth.

Activity: Count the sets of rings in a wood slice to learn the age of the tree or the branch. Slices can often be seen on maintained nature trails where fallen trees have been cut to make way for the path. Notice the size and shape of the rings. Draw them in your nature journal and write about what you find.

- By counting the ring pairs, can you tell how old this tree is? If your sample is from a branch, do the rings tell you how old the whole tree is? (No, it can only tell how old the branch is.)

- Are all the rings the same size? Can you see years of favorable conditions? Stressed conditions?

- Are there any lopsided rings? By looking around, can you see what could have been the cause?

- These rings make the beautiful wood grain we see in furniture. Can you find some examples in your home?

Diagram a Wood Slice

Get to know the inner anatomy of a tree

Background: A wood slice contains different sections of growth. The dark central rings are the heartwood. They are the oldest and are no longer living, but they give the tree strength. The sapwood rings, those surrounding the heartwood, transport water and nutrients up and down the tree. The ring closest to the bark is the actively growing ring, called the cambium. On the outside, the tree has bark to protect itself from animals, insects, and weather that may cause damage.

Activity: Look at a wood slice or freshly cut stump and locate the parts: heartwood (darker center rings), sapwood (lighter outer rings), cambium (ring closest to the bark), and bark. Draw the slice and label the parts in your nature journal.

Biggest and Smallest

See the variety of size in leaves

While on a nature walk, collect the largest and the smallest tree leaves you can find. As you go, compare your finds with new candidates, keeping only the biggest and smallest ones. Try to choose full-size mature leaves, not those just emerging from buds. Compare the leaf to others on the same tree to see if the leaf is the typical size for that tree type.

At the end of your walk, trace the biggest leaf on a page of your nature journal (or as much as you can, letting the outline trail off the edges). Then trace the smallest leaf in the very middle. Identify both in your field guide and label them.

- Are large leaves always found on large trees and small leaves on small trees, or is it unrelated?
- Are the large and small leaves of similar thicknesses, or are they different?

Crack Open Seeds

Investigate the makeup of tree seeds, use tools to crack seeds

Background: Tree seeds are similar to garden seeds in many ways. They have a protective outer coating and contain everything necessary to send out a root and a shoot when growing conditions are right. Some seeds need to go through a cold winter to trigger this process. All need moisture to soften the shell. The inner substance absorbs water and swells until it breaks through.

Most seeds will not grow into trees. They may be eaten by birds, squirrels, or insects. Others become homes for insect larvae, whose parents deposit eggs in the nutritious and safe capsule. Many will lay fallow on ground that is too dry and inhospitable. Some may germinate but be eaten or damaged as a tender seedling. A seed that avoids all of these fates rises slowly, year after year, into a great tree to produce seeds of its own, continuing the cycle.

Activity: Collect acorns, pine cones, nuts, maple "helicopters," and other tree seeds you come across. Check them over for holes or damage. These could indicate an insect living inside.

The seed contains everything it needs to grow a tree: instructions for growing, cells that are ready to form the first root, stem, and set of leaves, and enough food to sustain itself until it can start producing energy. Have everyone guess what the seeds look like inside then use a hammer or nutcracker to open them. Draw and write about it in your nature journal.

- Do all seeds have the same amount of protection? What are the benefits of a harder shell? What are the disadvantages?
- What takes up the most space inside the seed?
- Can you see the root, stem, and first leaves yet? What can you see?
- What is similar about all the seeds? What is different?
- Can you think of tree seeds that we eat? What part do we eat?

Sprout a Tree

See firsthand how trees grow from seeds

Plant a tree seed and monitor it as it sprouts. Maple tree seeds are especially easy to grow. Seeds that naturally fall from trees in the spring usually sprout in a few weeks. Seeds that are not ready until Fall come up in the spring, requiring a cold dormant time to germinate.

Draw the parent tree and a seed in your nature journal. Open the seed to see what is inside. Make notes in your nature journal.

Back at home, plant the seeds in the ground or outside in a pot, simulating nature as much as possible. Plant them whole at a shallow depth in moist soil. Cover them with a layer of leaves and let nature take its course.

In your journal, mark the date you planted. When the sprouts emerge, draw one and date it.

Sprouting a Tree Seed

Parent Tree	Tree Seed	Sprout

Date Planted: Date Sprouted:

- A tree is considered a seedling until it is 3 feet/1 meter high. What does a tree seedling look like when it first emerges? What do the second set of leaves look like?

- How is the seeding similar to its parent tree? How is it different?

- What date did the seedlings emerge? Did all of them come up? Was it at the same time?

- What weather conditions helped them know the time was right to grow?

Fall Spectrum

Figure out the order leaves change color, collect information and make conclusions

Background: Many deciduous trees in temperate and continental climates turn beautiful colors as they transition to winter. The tree prepares for the drop in temperature by shutting down its leaves and storing energy in its roots. A scab forms near the stem of each leaf, creating a block from the rest of the tree. Over time, the leaf dries out and loses its green color as its chlorophyll breaks down and displays yellows, oranges, reds, purple, or browns. Wind and gravity may cause the leaves to fall, leaving only a scar where it was once attached. Some trees hold onto their browned leaves until new growth pushes them off in the spring.

Activity: Collect leaves from a color-changing tree like a maple. Find leaves and arrange them in the full spectrum, changing from green to brown, looking closely to figure out which order the color change happens. Line them up, starting with a fully green leaf, then place one that is mostly green with some changing, etc, all the way to a fully brown leaf. Your spectrum may be complex like green-yellow-orange-red-brown or more simple like green-red-brown. Illustrate the color change process in your nature journal.

- In each leaf, how does the color change happen: from the tip or the stem, from the veins or the leaf edges, or is it random? Do all the leaves change color in the same way?

- On the tree, do the leaves first change from the top or the bottom? The inner leaves or the outer? Or is it random?

- Do the leaves feel different as they change further down the color spectrum? How do fully green leaves compare to fully brown leaves?

Leaf Rubbings

Consider the role of leaf veins, record leaf textures

Background: Leaves have a central vein flowing from the stem out to many branching veins that grow thinner as they spread across the leaf. This system delivers water and nutrients to the leaves and transports the energy that the leaf makes back to the main part of the tree. The veins also give the leaf structure to keep it upright and spread toward the sunlight.

Activity: Place a leaf under your nature journal page and rub the side of a crayon to record the veins and textures. Identify the tree/shrub it came from. Look closely at the paths the veins take. Crack open the central vein and look inside it. Write your observations next to the rubbing.

- Can you explain, in your own words, what veins are for?

- Do the veins get thicker or thinner as they move away from the center of the tree? Trace the path with your finger.

- Do leaf veins remind you of anything else in nature? (Tree trunks with branches and twigs, waterway systems like rivers and creeks, arteries and veins in human bodies.)

Diagram a Leaf

Get to know the anatomy of a leaf

Draw or trace a leaf in your nature journal and label the parts: petiole (stem), node (bottom of the stem, where it connects to the tree), stipules (leaflike parts coming from the node), midrib (center vein), veins, tip, and blade (edge).

Needles vs. Leaves

Notice the similarities and differences between evergreen needles and deciduous leaves

Background: All leaves, whether they be the flat-veined variety of deciduous trees or the thin sharp needles of an evergreen, have the same job: they take in sunlight and carbon dioxide from the atmosphere and use it along with water and nutrients from the soil to produce food for their tree. The process is called photosynthesis. This requires chlorophyll, a green pigment, and thus both types of leaves are green.

Despite having the same function, needles and broad leaves are built differently. Evergreens are designed to survive cold weather, with thin needles held closer to their trunk bodies than the stretched-out, branching deciduous varieties. The needles often have a protective, wax-like coating. Their veins are buried inside, while broad leaves have veins along their surfaces. Evergreen needles are built to last a long time, while deciduous leaves serve their purpose very well for the season, die off, and are replaced the next spring.

Activity: Collect a fresh deciduous leaf and a fresh branch with needles. Look at each closely and note their similarities and differences in color, texture, and shape. Write up your observations in your nature journal and illustrate them with examples.

- Feel a needle and a leaf. How do they compare?
- How does each connect to its tree?
- What shape is a needle? What shape is a leaf?
- How do needles smell? How do leaves smell?
- Break open a needle and rip a leaf. What is similar? What is different?

Pollen vs. Seed Cones

Understand the difference between the two types of pine cones

Background: Most conifers (cone-bearing trees) produce two kinds of pine cones on the same tree: one contains the pollen while the other develops the seed. In the spring, the pollen cones open to allow the wind to carry the pollen to the seed cones. The seed cone then develops seeds and releases them when they are mature.

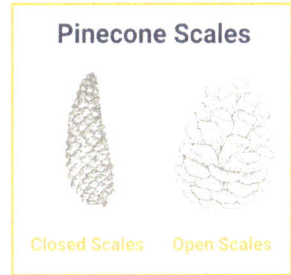

Pinecone Scales

Closed Scales   Open Scales

Activity: Visit a conifer in late spring or early summer. Look for a pollen cone, which is small and soft. They may be covered in a yellow dust, the pollen. After a few weeks, these cones will wither and fall off the tree. Next, find a seed cone, which is the larger, harder, more familiar shape. These cones remain on the tree, opening and closing their scales depending on the moisture in the air. Once fully developed, the seeds fall from the cone to be transported by gravity, wind, water, or animals to grow into full trees if the conditions are right. Open the cone to see if you can spot the seeds. Each scale has two seeds attached to it.

Draw both types of cones in your nature journal and write about their roles. Draw a seed if you were able to find one.

Diagram an Evergreen Branch

Get to know the anatomy of an evergreen branch

Draw a small section of an evergreen branch in your nature journal. Label the parts: twig, bud scar (ring-like marks on the twig from previous needles), fascicle (group of 2-5 needles), fascicle sheath, needles, bud/immature needles (soft, brighter green cluster on the ends of the branches), and pine cone (seeds).

Evergreen Growth

Figure out how evergreen trees grow

Background: Evergreens use the same needles year after year, but not forever. Old needles die, and new ones are grown, but not all at once like the leaves of deciduous trees. The individual dying needles may turn orange or brown before falling off, but the tree remains green overall. New needles may be brighter in color and softer in feel than the older growth.

Activity: Visit an evergreen tree in the spring or summer. Collect a newly grown needle, a mature needle, a fading needle, and a dead needle from the ground. Illustrate these examples in your nature journal and label them.

- Try bending each sample and compare. Which are the most flexible? Which are brittle?

- Do needles seem to grow longer and longer as they age or do they mature to stay the same size?

- Where does the new growth appear? Where are dying needles situated? Do you see twigs that have no needles at all? Why do you think it happens this way?

Resin and Sap

Understand what resin and sap are, learn how they serve their trees

Background: Sap is a clear, watery liquid that flows through deciduous trees and evergreens. Tree roots pull water and nutrients up from the soil, and the sapwood transports it out to the branches and leaves. This keeps the leaves and needles from wilting and it supplies them in their job of making food for the tree through photosynthesis. In the leaves, the sap is loaded with this sweet energy and it flows back out through the veins to the rest of the tree to feed it. People discovered this treasure long ago. Maple trees continue to be drilled to this day, collecting its sugary sap and boiling it down to produce sweet maple syrup.

Resin is quite different in form and function. It is produced by some varieties of evergreen trees and is thick and amber-colored. Some scientists think it holds waste for the tree, while others think it is designed primarily as a protective "glue" to help the tree heal from the damage caused by insects, disease, weather, or animals. Resin hardens when exposed to air, so people use it for jewelry, making surfaces more durable and waterproof, and as an ingredient in some chemicals.

Activity: Observe sap firsthand by visiting a maple syrup farm in late winter. If not possible, watch a video online. Look at sap dripping into the collection buckets and see the boiling process. Describe and illustrate how maple sap turns into syrup in your nature journal.

Look for resin on pines, cedars, spruces, redwoods, firs, yews, junipers, or larches. This sticky material oozes out from cracks in the bark and may slowly roll down the tree. Smell it. Touch it. Draw and write about what you notice in your nature journal.

- Why is sap watery? Why does it have to be that way to help the tree?

- Can you find hardened resin? Is there any that is still sticky? What will happen over time?

"Sunshine is delicious, rain is refreshing, wind braces us up, snow is exhilarating; there is really no such thing as bad weather, only different kinds of good weather."

John Ruskin

Weather & Climate

Weather and Climate

The weather is the outside conditions at a specific time, including temperature, precipitation (rain, snow, hail, sleet), sunshine/cloudiness, humidity, wind, and atmospheric pressure. At extremes, these factors result in storms. Heavy rains pool into floods. Areas of high air pressure collide with areas of low air pressure to cause destructive winds. Extreme heat with a lack of rain causes drought.

When these elements of weather are averaged over about 30 years, they describe the climate for an area. Climate conditions determine what kinds of plants and animals can live and thrive in a region, resulting in areas looking and feeling very different from each other.

Learn more about the weather and climate at the National Weather Service website: https://www.weather.gov

Field Guide:

National Audubon Society Field Guide to Weather

Books (Available free on archive.org):

Weather Words and What They Mean by Gail Gibbons

Weather Forecasting by Gail Gibbons

The Reasons for Seasons by Gail Gibbons

Anywhere in the World: The Story of Plant and Animal Adaptation by Irma Webber

Reading Radar

See how radar works, learn how radar helps predict the weather

Background: One way weather scientists predict coming rain and snow is through a technology called radar. They send beams from the weather station into the atmosphere. These bounce off clouds and precipitation and return to the ground where detectors read them. In general, the stronger the return signal, the more precipitation there is. Meteorologists monitor the thickness and movement of these weather masses to estimate which areas will get precipitation and how much. This is only one factor in predicting weather, as large groups of migrating birds also show up on radar, indistinguishable from clouds. For a more in-depth understanding of radar, read about it at https://www.weather.gov/mkx/using-radar.

Activity: Find out where your closest radar station is. Watch a local weather report, use an app like NOAA, or visit a website like https://radar.weather.gov to track the movement of an incoming storm. Compare the real-time radar readings to what you see when you look out your window. Write about the process in your nature journal. Draw a simple map with your home and the closest weather station marked.

- Explain how radar works in your own words.
- Why do you think there are not weather stations in every city? (Each station can monitor a wide area, the instruments are expensive, and the stations need to be staffed by experts.)

Prediction vs. Actual

Learn how meteorologists make weather predictions, test the accuracy of a forecast for one week, collect and analyze data

Background: Weather forecasters use a variety of tools to help them predict what the weather will be like in the coming days. We use this in deciding when to go to the beach or plant a garden. However, these predictions are only "educated guesses". The weather scientists collect measurements and information, but they cannot know for sure what will happen. There are a lot of factors that can change. Read about the tools forecasters use to predict the weather in a book or on a website like https://www.noaa.gov/stories/6-tools-our-meteorologists-use-to-forecast-weather.

Activity: For one week, compare the weather forecast to what actually happens. Start by making a table like this in your nature journal or printing it from naturestudycollective.com:

Weather Prediction vs. Actual

	High Temp		Cloudiness		Precipitation	
Date	Forecast	Actual	Forecast	Actual	Forecast	Actual

At the beginning of the week, record information from the weather report in the "Forecast" columns. As the week goes on, fill out what actually happened. Check the current conditions each day at the same time, preferably at lunch or in the afternoon for the warmest temperature.

At the end of the week, analyze how accurate the forecast was.

- Was the forecast spot on, generally accurate, hit or miss, or totally wrong?
- Did the forecast get more or less accurate as the week went on, farther from the time they made the prediction?

Temperature Graph

Learn how to measure temperature, see how temperature changes day by day, collect and analyze data, create a graph

Track the temperature each day for a week. Collect the data on a table like the one here in your nature journal. A printable is available on naturestudycollective.com. Each day at the same time, such as at lunch or during science class, go outside to feel the temperature. Guess what the temperature is in degrees. Then, read an outdoor thermostat or consult a weather app and record it in your nature journal.

Temperature for One Week

Monday: _____
Tuesday: _____
Wednesday: _____
Thursday: _____
Friday: _____
Saturday: _____
Sunday: _____

WEATHER AND CLIMATE

At the end of the week, graph the temperature in your nature journal. Paste graph paper on the page and format it like the one below. A printable is available on naturestudycollective.com. Define your y-axis (vertical) scale by labeling every 5 or 10 degrees to fit your data. Chart the temperatures by plotting your points. Connect them with straight lines to show the trend.

Temperature by Day

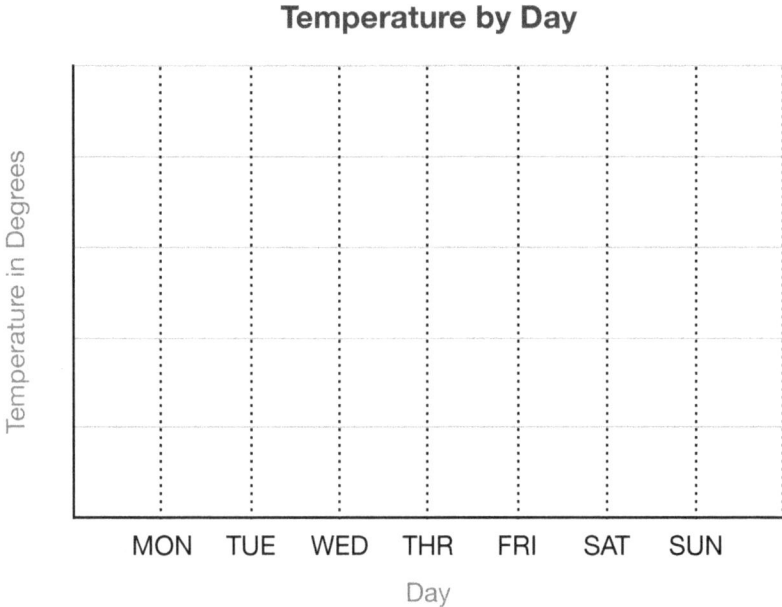

- Did the week get colder, warmer, or vary day by day?
- Could you tell just by feeling what the temperature was approximately? Exactly?

Local Storms

Become aware of storms that can occur in your home area, learn how people have adapted to endure storms

Background: There are many forms of severe weather: tornados, earthquakes, thunderstorms, floods, hurricanes, blizzards, hail, freezing rain, and wildfire conditions. Depending on where you live, some of these are more common than others. Visit the Storm Prediction Center on the National Weather Service website for current severe weather alerts: https://www.spc.noaa.gov.

All homes have a roof and walls to keep out rain and wind. In cooler climates, homes have furnaces that keep the people inside warm. In areas where specific storms are common, the homes are built with extra protections as well.

Activity: Talk about which kind of storms are likely/possible in your area. Then walk around and point out special protections your home has and describe what they are for. Examples include a lightning rod, sump pump, drainage landscaping, earthquake-resistant construction, hurricane shutters, tornado shelter/basement, power generator, wood-burning fireplace, sloped roof, and insulated pipes. Write up a nature journal entry with sketches.

- Which types of storms can hit your area? Which types are impossible or very unlikely?

- How can you know when severe weather is approaching?

- What is your family's plan for staying safe in dangerous storms?

Water Cycle Demo

Demonstrate how evaporation, condensation, and precipitation occurs in the environment, understand the water cycle

Background: As water is warmed, it turns from a liquid into a vapor. This is called "evaporation." When we hang a wet towel in the sunshine, it will be dry when we take it down later. The water did not disappear; it turned from liquid water to water vapor, the gas form of water, and it floated into the air.

After rainfall, the water goes back up into the atmosphere in the same way. As it warms, it turns into water vapor. This is lighter than air and thus rises high into the atmosphere. The higher it goes, the cooler the conditions are. It then turns back into water droplets. These cling to dust, or "condenses," forming clouds above us. More and more water is attracted until they are heavier than the air. They then fall back down to the ground as "precipitation," rain or snow, depending on the temperature. We call this the "water cycle" because it repeats over and over.

Activity: Simulate the water cycle on your kitchen counter. Pour a few inches/centimeters of boiling water in a clear jar. This is like sun-warmed groundwater. Cover the jar with plastic wrap and place a bowl of ice on top, mimicking the cool upper atmosphere. Watch what happens. The warm water evaporates and is visible as a misty cloud. The droplets then condense on the plastic wrap, as they do with the dust in our atmosphere. Over time, you can see that the water collects until it drips back down, much like the precipitation of rain and snow.

Explain the water cycle on a page in your nature journal using a diagram and written notes.

Rain Gauge

Monitor rainfall and learn how it is measured, practice reading a scale

Make a rain gauge using a straight-sided jar and monitor the precipitation that falls in your own backyard. Use a permanent marker and a ruler to mark the jar every inch, starting from the bottom. Place it outside in an open area, away from buildings and trees. This will make your readings more accurate. After a rain, check your gauge and compare it to the official rainfall reading for your city. This reading is available on weather.gov for your location.

- How much rain did you get?

- How can you read the measurement if it is above or below a line you marked?

- Did you get more or less rain than the official number for your area? Why could this be different? (The water falling in each specific spot varies.)

Cloud Types

Be able to recognize the basic cloud types when looking at the sky

Background: There are four primary cloud types. Cirrus clouds are high and wispy. The name comes from the Latin for "hair." Cumulus clouds are puffy, derived from the Latin meaning "pile." Stratus clouds blanket the sky and the name

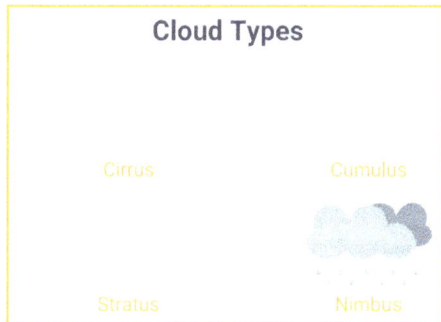

Cloud Types

Cirrus   Cumulus

Stratus   Nimbus

comes from the Latin for "layer." When these clouds are at ground level, we have fog. Nimbus clouds are those that are actively raining or snowing. The name means "rain-bearing" in Latin.

Activity: Look at the sky each day for one week and identify the clouds you see. There may be more than one type present. In your nature journal, write the date and draw the clouds and label them. Write "none" if the sky is clear.

- Can you describe each of the four cloud types?

- Which cloud types were most common during your observation?

Rainbow Spotting

Learn how rainbows are formed, know where to spot them in the sky

Background: Rainbows appear when white light from the sun breaks through the clouds and bounces off water droplets in the air of a rainy day. The light separates into its full-color spectrum: red, orange, yellow, green, blue, indigo, and violet. Since it is made by the reflected light, rainbows are always found directly opposite of the sun in the sky.

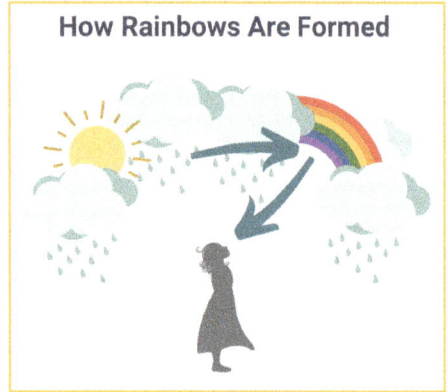

How Rainbows Are Formed

Activity: Demonstrate how rainbows are formed using a hose with a spray attachment or sprinkler in the backyard. Stand with your back to the sun and look at the spray. Change your angle slightly until you see the rainbow. Move side to side to see that the rainbow moves with you.

Diagram this process in your nature journal, using words to explain.

- What elements do you need for a rainbow to form?

- Why does the rainbow move when you do? (A rainbow is not an object in itself, but rather the effect of the light from your view.)

- What colors are in a rainbow? Did you see the colors always in the same order? Read more about color wavelengths in a book or online if your students are interested in learning more.

- While outside, can you point to where a rainbow would be if there was enough moisture in the air right now?

Snowflake Viewing

See the beauty, detail, and uniqueness of snowflakes, understand how snowflakes are formed

Background: A snowflake forms by a water droplet freezing on a dust or pollen particle in the atmosphere. This always forms a central hexagon shape because of the chemical makeup of water. More water freezes onto this initial crystal as it falls through the atmosphere, symmetrically adding "arms" to the design. The colder the conditions are, the more intricate the pattern becomes. The snowflake may change shape many times before it finally lands and we are able to see it.

Snowflakes

Hexagon Center with Six Branches

Activity: Set a dark-colored scarf outside while it is snowing to catch some flakes. They will rest on the fibers, usually without being damaged. Look at a single snowflake up close with a magnifying glass. Re-create it in your nature journal.

- How many points does your snowflake have?

- Do you see any hexagons?

- Is it perfectly symmetrical? If not, can you see where it has been altered?

- Compare one flake to another. Are they exactly the same? How are they similar? Different?

Measure Snowfall

Learn how snowfall is measured, practice reading a ruler

Background: As snowflakes fall to the Earth, they land on each other in great numbers, creating a pile of indiscernible white. They initially form in the very cold high atmosphere. If the lower air is warmer, they may melt slightly and stick together to become a wet, dense, and heavy snow. If the lower air is frigid, the snowflakes are stiffer and stack lightly on each other.

Activity: Take a tape measure outside and plunge it into the snow with the 0 in/cm side touching the ground. Read the height measurement to see how much snow there is. The sample spot must be undisturbed, on flat ground, and clear of overhead trees or buildings that may interfere with the free-falling snow.

- What would cause the snow depth to increase in coming days? (More snowfall)
- What factors would cause the snow depth to decrease in coming days? (Temperatures above 32°F/0°C causing melt or a force like wind displacing the snow)
- How could a taller measurement actually be made up of fewer snowflakes? (Colder snowflakes stack higher on each other)

Season Changes

Investigate how nature changes with the seasons

Visit a favorite nature area once per season. Designate a page in your nature journal, dividing it into quarters and labeling it with "Fall," "Winter," "Spring," and "Summer." Write or draw the differences you notice in nature. Look for which plants are growing, what the trees look like, which birds are flying overhead, and what the water levels are.

- How has nature responded to the changing conditions?
- In which season do you like to visit this spot best?

Identify Climates

Learn about the Earth's major climate zones, imagine what it is like living in different climates

Background: The Earth has five primary climates. Listed roughly in order from the equator to the poles, they are: tropical, dry, temperate, continental, and polar. Tropical regions are warm and humid because they are located near the equator where the sun's rays are more direct year-round. Dry zones have comparatively little precipitation and their high heat makes moisture evaporate quickly. Temperate areas have warm summers and mild winters, often because their temperatures are kept more moderate by a large body of water. Continental places, in contrast, have more extreme temperature shifts of hot summers and cold winters. Polar climates are farthest from the equator and are cold most of the year.

Activity: In your nature journal, make a list of people you know who live in different locations. Read through the descriptions of the climate zones and write the climate for each: tropical, dry, temperate, continental, and polar.

- Which climate do you live in?

- Have you visited an alternate climate? How was it different?

- What would you enjoy about living in each of the climates? What would be some disadvantages?

"If a child is to keep alive his inborn sense of wonder, he needs the companionship of at least one adult who can share it, rediscovering with him the joy, excitement, and mystery of the world we live in."

Rachel Carson

Wildflowers

Wildflowers

Wildflowers are plants that grow readily on their own without human tending. In places they are not wanted, they are called "weeds" and people fight mightily to prevent them from overtaking the lawn and garden. Wildflowers are generally hardy and self-propagating, feeding hosts of insects and providing shelter for small mammals. You may find wildflowers in sidewalk cracks, along roadsides, in vast fields of untouched natural areas, and in any otherwise unused land. Wildflowers are proof that there is beauty everywhere.

Field Guides:

National Audubon Society Field Guide to Wildflowers: Eastern Region

National Audubon Society Field Guide to Wildflowers: Western Region

Books (Available free on archive.org):

The How and Why Wonder Book of Wild Flowers by Grace Ferguson

Look at a Flower by Anne Ophelia Dowden

Travelers All: The Story of How Plants Go Places by Irma Webber

Seeds and Seed Travels by Bertha Morris Parker

Little Wanderers by Margaret Morely

Weeds by Dorothy Childs Hogner

Rainbow Collection

Explore the variety of wildflower colors

Make it your mission to find one wildflower blossom in each color of the rainbow: red, orange, yellow, green, blue, indigo, and violet. In-between shades can be included to build a gradual spectrum. Green-petalled wildflowers exist but are rare. Use an immature bloom or grass in that slot. If picking is allowed, mount the petals in your nature journal in the rainbow-spectrum order and cover with packing tape. If not, draw your finds instead. Identify each wildflower and label it.

Study 12

Learn to recognize 12 different kinds of wildflowers

Choose a new wildflower to study each week over the term/semester. Use a field guide or nature ID app to learn its name. Draw the bloom in your nature journal and write up everything you notice about the plant.

You could press the flower for two weeks and then mount it in your journal beside your entry or include it immediately by carefully flattening it and sealing it on the page with packing tape.

- Where was the wildflower found? About how many of this type are living there?

- Count and measure the plant. How tall does it stand? What is the diameter of the flower head? How many petals does it have?

- Look at another wildflower of this same type. Are they identical? Does this plant always have the same amount of petals? Do they always have the same number of leaves?

- Look at the leaves. How many leaves are on each stem? Are the leaves opposite each other like a mirror, do they alternate like footsteps, or are they all in a bunch? Are the leaf edges smooth, zig-zagged, or rounded lobes?

- Where are the seeds located? What do they look like? What is inside each seed?

Diagram a Wildflower

Get to know the anatomy of a wildflower

Background: Every living organism is designed to create offspring. Wildflowers produce seeds to replicate themselves. For a successful seed, pollen from the anther must get to the stigma, either from the same plant or from correlating plants of the same species. However, flowers cannot move themselves. How then can this happen?

The two most common ways are wind and living pollinators. Some flowers rely on wind to blow pollen produced by the anther through the air where some may land on the stigma. Living pollinators like insects, birds, and bats go from flower to flower eating the pollen or sipping the nectar. As they do so, they unintentionally transport pollen.

Activity: Analyze a flower and find the parts: stalk, sepal (small green flaps at the top of the stalk), and petals.

Then find the "female" parts of the flower which develop the seed: ovary (ball where the seeds are kept), style (center tube connected to the ovary), and stigma (top of the style).

Find the "male" parts of the flower which fertilize the seed: filaments (small stalks that hold up the anthers), and anthers (oval-shaped sacs that produce and hold the pollen).

Draw the flower and label all the parts in your nature journal. Explain how pollination works in your own words.

Bouquet

Appreciate the diverse beauty of wildflowers

Create a bouquet of wildflowers collected from a nature preserve, a local park with an un-mown section, a nature trail, or a country roadside. Some areas may be protected, so be sure you are allowed to pick the flowers.

Bring scissors and a mason jar or vase filled partly with water to hold your bouquet. Choose an odd number of big main blooms first- 3 or 5 work well. Cut these to the desired size, shake out any bugs, and place them in your container. Fill in the gaps with a variety of medium-sized supporting flowers. Once in place, supplement with small fillers of tiny blooms, seed pods, and anything else that catches your interest. Surround your collection with greenery cut a bit shorter than the blossoms.

Draw your creation in your nature journal. Learn the names of the wildflowers using a field guide or nature ID app and label them in your journal.

- How are wildflowers similar to flowers bought from a shop?
- How are they different?

Classify Wildflower Blooms

Understand the differentiating characteristics of wildflowers, practice classification

Visit an area with a variety of wildflowers and classify the plants by flower shape. As you look at each blossom, decide if it is a "ray," "trumpet/bell," "cluster," or "irregular" flower.

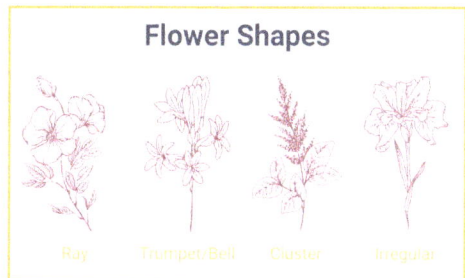

Flower Shapes

Ray   Trumpet/Bell   Cluster   Irregular

- Are the petals mostly flat and arranged around a single center? This would be a "ray" flower.
- Do the petals form a tube? This would be a "trumpet" or "bell" flower.
- Are there lots of petals and centers arranged in a tight bunch? This would be a "cluster" flower.
- Are the petals asymmetrical with some pointing upward and some pointing downward? This would be an "irregular" flower.

Look for an example of each of the four flower shapes and draw them in your nature journal.

Youngest to Oldest

Witness the life cycle of a wildflower bloom

Visit a patch of wildflowers and see if you can find examples of the full bloom cycle for one kind of flower. First, look for a young plant that has not opened its blooms yet. Next, search for a flower that is just starting to emerge. Then, find an example of a fully open, mature flower. Afterward, see if there are any fading blossoms. Finally, look for a plant that has lost all its petals.

In your nature journal, draw or press an example of each stage as a timeline of the bloom cycle. Under each, write your observations.

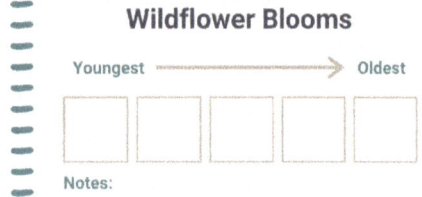

Wildflower Blooms

Youngest ———————➤ Oldest

Notes:

- What does the flower head look like before it has blossomed? How can you tell a blossom is developing?

- How do the petals open: all at once or petal by petal? Which petals open first?

- What does the fully open flower look like? What is in the center? What does this flower smell like? Does it smell differently than an immature, unopened bloom?

- How can you tell when petals are dying? What happens to them? Can you see any fallen petals on the ground?

- Once the petals are gone, what does the flower look like? Can you tell where the seeds are?

Petal Variety

Appreciate the diversity of flower petal shapes among wildflowers

Background: Wildflowers come in a wide variety of shapes and forms. Some are the classic shape of 5 oval petals spreading out from a round center, but flowers can also look like hanging bells, tiny-petaled clusters, star-shaped points, or deep funnels. Some have a single bloom at the top of a stem, while others have several offshoots splayed in various directions. The individual petals may be round or pointed, ridged or flat, large or tiny. Some flowers are neatly symmetrical; others are beautifully irregular.

Activity: Visit an area with wildflowers and collect as many different petals as you can find. Tape or draw one petal from each type in your nature journal. Write about the variety of colors, shapes, sizes, designs, and textures you found.

Wildflower Field Guide

Become familiar with all the wildflowers on a nature trail, practice using a field guide to identity wildflowers, observe closely to decide between similar types of flowers

Create a custom wildflower field guide for a favorite nature trail. Walk along slowly and spot wildflowers. If picking is allowed, select one of each type you come across and mount it to a page in your nature journal. Carefully flatten the bloom and cover it with a smooth layer of packing tape. If picking is not allowed, create an accurate drawing instead. Use a nature app or field guide to identify the wildflower's name and label it in your journal. Look closely at the number of petals, the shape of the leaves, and the measurements to ensure you have chosen the correct variety. Date the top of each page to have a record of when these flowers bloom.

If there are many different wildflowers in the area, this could be a project you work on a bit each week. Also, some wildflowers are only in bloom for a short time. You could do a new field guide for each season.

When finished, you will have gotten to know many wildflowers and produced a beautiful collection of those that live there. Share this guide with grandparents or friends and invite them to come along on your next hike to spot these flowers for themselves along your trail.

Seed Dispersal Methods

Explore the different ways wildflower seeds travel from the parent plant

Background: Wildflower seeds are formed on the mother plant and are sent off to grow into a plant of their own. Wildflowers cannot move, so they use a variety of natural forces.

WILDFLOWERS

Activity: Divide your journal page into five sections and label them:
"Wind," "Gravity," "Water," "Eaten by Animals," and "Sticking to Animals." Analyze each seed you find and tape it in the appropriate section.

Seed Dispersal Methods

Wind   Gravity   Water

Eaten by Animals   Sticking to Animals

Wind: Some plants grow seeds that are equipped to sail in the breeze. As the wind blows, the seeds are carried from the plant to new places to start life on their own. To see if a seed is dispersed by wind, toss it up into the air to see if it floats.

- How is this seed designed to travel in the wind?
- Which part is the actual seed? Which part is for its dispersal?

Gravity: Other seeds use gravity and simply fall where they may. Wind, rain, or passing animals knock the seeds off the plant to the soil below. These seeds fall relatively straight down when dropped.

- How are gravity seeds designed differently from the other types of seeds you found?
- Since these seeds scatter very near their parent plant, look to see if there are several of these plants growing beside each other.

Water: Wildflowers growing near streams or rivers may rely on the current to carry its seeds to new homes. Drop the seed into the water to see if it floats.

- After falling into the water, where do the seeds go? Are there more of these plants there?

Eaten by Animals: Some wildflowers embed their seeds in tasty berries. Birds and other animals eat these and later deposit the seed in a new location with their droppings.

- Which part of this plant is edible to the animal? How does the appearance make an animal want to eat it? Does it have a vibrant color or a pungent smell?
- Find the actual seed. How is it situated on the plant? How is it protected against the digestive system of the animal?

Sticking to Animals: Seeds covered in tiny hooks get stuck in the fur or feathers of passing animals, hitching a ride to a new location. The animal pulls them off, or they dry out and lose grip. These seeds easily stick to our clothing as well. Test it on your shirt. Velcro was inspired by this natural design.

- Look closely at the hooks. What are they like? How are they attached to the seed?

Plant Wildflower Seeds

Observe the full cycle of a wildflower seed growing into a full plant, understand how nature grows plants, document your observations, collect data and draw a graph

Collect wildflower seeds and plant them in a garden or in a pot at home. Many seeds are ready in late summer or fall. You can tell they are mature when they have turned brown and can be easily removed from the flower or pod. Wildflowers typically produce an abundance of seeds, so isolate just a few for planting.

Simulate nature in your planting space. Press the seeds into the soil shallowly and cover them with a thin layer of soil, moisten them with water, and top with leaves. Write the name of the wildflower in permanent marker on a popsicle stick and slide it into the dirt nearby.

WILDFLOWERS

Some seeds may sprout after a few days, while others may have to go through the natural process of overwintering, waiting for the ideal growing conditions of spring. Seeds that overwinter can be left for the snow and rain to tend to them. They will break out of dormancy to grow when the temperatures are just right.

Create a nature journal entry for each plant. Write the flower name at the top and list where you found it. Tape a seed on the page. Leave space for drawing the plant in its growing stages. Paste a graph paper sheet to chart the plant height over time.

Wildflower Growth

Name of the Plant:
Where Found:
Date Planted:

Seed   Sprout   Plant   Growth

Set the scale based on the mature height listed in your field guide.

- How do the seeds look similar to each other? How are they different?
- How many seeds do you estimate each wildflower produces?
- Do the plants look similar or different from each other when they first sprout? How do the second set of leaves compare to the first?
- How long does it take for the plant to produce a flower? What does the bud look like before blooming?
- How long does the blossom last?
- How long does it take a plant to go from being planted as a seed to producing fully mature seeds of its own?

Herbarium

Notice every detail of a wildflower, press and mount plants

A herbarium is a collection of plants preserved for scientific study and has been done for hundreds of years as a hobby. Create a herbarium of wildflowers on a theme: those found in a specific season, those that grow in your backyard, or create a collection of your favorites.

Use a hand shovel to carefully lift a whole wildflower plant out of the ground intact. You will want undamaged examples of its roots, stem, leaves, blossoms, and seeds. Gently shake out the soil from the roots. Flatten the flower head and the leaves to preserve the details. You may want to include another flower head pressed in a side view to show that angle as well. Include some seeds from this plant or a neighboring one.

Dry your plant in a flower press or a thick book between sheets of smooth white copy paper. If the specimen is too tall to fit in your press or on your page, snip it into segments.

After two weeks, mount the flower on a page in your journal, securing the stems with thin strips of tape. Label with the plant name, date, and location you found it. Some petals may lose color. If that happens, make a note of the original beside the blossom. Write up any other details you want to remember about your specimen.

Grass Study

Get to know the anatomy of grass

Background: Grasses are found alongside wildflowers, and though they do not have petals and showy blooms, they have a lot in common. There is a wide variety, but all are unmistakably grass, from the green blades we encourage to take over our lawns to the strong, tall stems that wave in meadow breezes.

Activity: Examine untrimmed grass closely. You may be surprised to see a plant more complex than the single blades hastily drawn on the ground of a picture. In un-mown fields, you can see that grass has a single stalk with blades jutting out from sheaths and bending gracefully. The tip contains the "flower," though in a unique way. Yet, it still contains seeds to propagate itself.

Illustrate these parts with accurate colors and describe the texture and form of the plant. Tape some seeds beside your entry. Next, dig up a small patch of grass and notice the threadlike roots. You may see new shoots arising from the roots, a "rhizome" system, which increases the range of this prolific plant. Add a below-ground view.

- What do grass roots look like? Do you see any new shoots growing from them? How do these help the plant?

- What is the texture of the grass stem? What shade of green is it? Is it all one color?

- How is the stem different from the blades? Break it open. What is it like inside?

- Describe the grass flower and seeds. About how many seeds are there?

Grass Collection

Learn about different types of grass

Background: We often think of grass as a single thing: a plant with green blades growing on the ground. However, there is a vast diversity of grasses found in nature. While they all have the same basic form, they can be quite different from each other in appearance and growing conditions. Some types do best carpeting damp forests while others grow vigorously in sunny fields.

Activity: Visit a nature area to collect the varieties of grass living there. Start looking right from the parking lot. Keep one blade of each type you discover. When you come upon a new specimen, compare it to the others you have already to see if it is unique or a repeat.

Draw each specimen in your nature journal, noting its colors, full height (if not mowed), blade thickness, texture, strength, and unique characteristics.

- Is all grass the same color? Is it the same shade?

- Are all the blades different thicknesses or about the same? For the same type, are the blades consistent?

- How tall does un-mown grass grow? Does it depend on the type?

- Is some grass easier to cut than others? What makes it so?

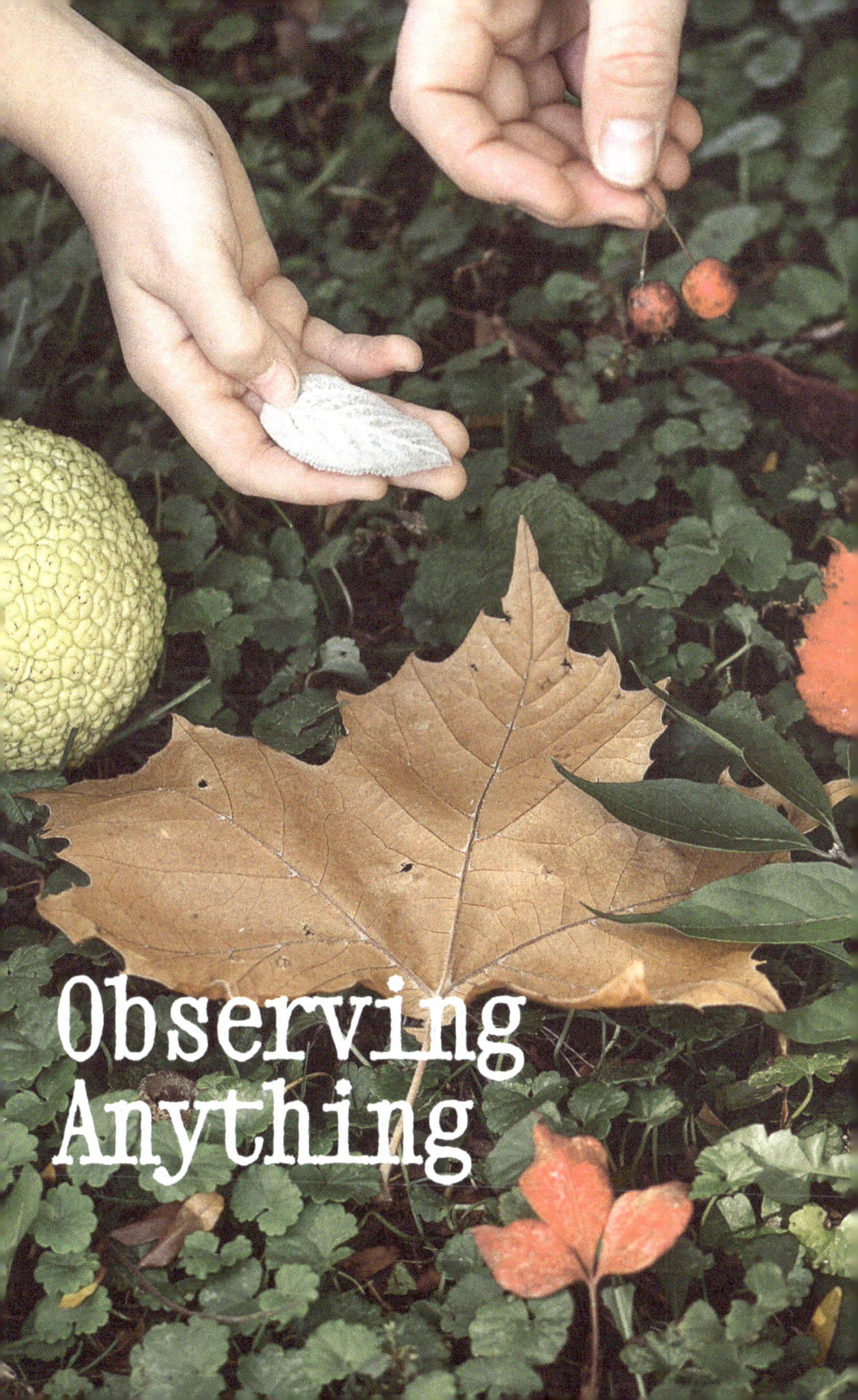

Observing
Anything

Observing Anything

This is a general collection of ideas for nature study, applicable across multiple subjects.

Senses

Use all five senses to collect information, exercise observing thoroughly, learn about a nature specimen

Find something in nature that you would like to study. Use your five senses to learn all you can about it. Look closely. Smell it. Feel it with your fingers. Shake it and listen. If you are sure it is edible, taste it. After you have noticed everything you can, record your findings in your nature journal. Show some aspects using pictures, describe other characteristics in words, and label with numbers anything that you can count and measure.

Field Guide Checkoff

Learn how to use a field guide for identification, get acquainted with local nature, develop a sense of what is common and rare, encourage ongoing awareness for nature sightings

Obtain a field guide for a nature topic and use it as a checklist, marking each entry when you see it in real life. This activity works well for butterflies, insects, trees, constellations, mammals, and wildflowers especially. Recommended field guides are listed for each category in this book.

If you choose to focus on birds, for example, you can add a checkmark and the date to the "robin" page when you spot them searching for worms in your yard, "red-tailed hawk" seen while driving along a country road, and "seagull" watched while swimming at the beach.

This simple activity will have you tuned in to nature all around. While marking, you learn how to use the field guide and connect the sighting with the name. Some things will be encountered again and again, becoming well known. Others are a rare treat.

Calendar of Firsts

Come to understand the general timing of nature, learn to create a data table, use these records to reference in anticipation of seasonal nature events

Keep track of when things happen for the first time throughout the year, such as the first snow, the first ducklings, and the first fireflies. Write these events on a calendar or as logged entries in a dedicated journal. Include the date, the event, and the location. (This activity is based on Charlotte Mason's "Calendars," described in "Home Education" on page 55.)

Calendar of Firsts

Date	Event	Location

Memory

Build observation skills through a simple game, use a field guide for identification

When your child finds something they want to know the name of, such as a bird, flower, insect, leaf, or mushroom, have them look closely and try to remember as much as possible about it. Once they are ready, hide the item and allow them to use a field guide to figure out what the name is. As they flip through the pages and consider the varieties, they will test how well they had paid attention. Once they have settled on the identification, compare the listing side by side to the actual item to see if they were right.

All Angles

Build thorough observation skills, learn about a nature specimen, use a magnification device

After finding a nature item, look at it from all angles: top, bottom, sides, front, and back. What do you notice? If possible, break it open to see what is inside. Use a magnifying glass or pocket microscope to see tiny details.

Record your findings in your nature journal. Draw the main view and use arrows pointing to smaller boxes that have alternate views or special details. Whatever you cannot communicate well with pictures, describe using words and numbers. It may be hard to illustrate the leathery texture of the seed pod, but you could easily communicate that with a note. Count what can be numbered: how many legs on the insect, speckles on the egg, thorns on the stem? Include as much information as you can in your entry.

Circle Game

Practice careful observation, take turns in a group, learn about a nature specimen

Pass around a nature specimen in a group/family. Each person should tell one thing they notice about it that no one else has already said. If someone can't think of anything, they are "out." The person who discovers the most is the "winner." This activity encourages attention to detail and everyone learns a lot about the nature item in the process. Choose any plant, animal, or insect that you can handle.

Nature Wreath

Appreciate the diversity and beauty of nature, use nature in an artistic activity

Bring a natural grapevine wreath with you while out in nature and work together as a group to weave wildflowers, seed pods, leaves, branches, moss, and whatever other beautiful things you find along the way. Make sure collecting is allowed in the nature area. When you get home, reinforce with hot glue if necessary and hang.

Vacations

Encounter nature areas different than your own

Trips can take us to new climates and regions, giving opportunity for nature experiences beyond our home sphere. Listed below are some ideas for making the most of these special times.

Wherever you go, look for nature centers and animal sanctuaries, which often teach about local wildlife. An internet search is an easy way to find places of interest. Many state and national parks have museums or centers that are worth visiting. Also, there are National Wildlife Refuge locations scattered across the United States. Find one near your vacation spot or road trip route using this map: https://www.fws.gov/refuges/find-a-wildlife-refuge/

Keep an ongoing family travel journal for your trips. Post photos, list the nature sites you visit, keep a record of new animals you see, mount interesting leaves and flowers, and have each family member create a nature journal entry. Over time, this will be a family treasure!

Bring along personal nature journals and field guides for free use. Lead by example, working in your own journal during downtimes.

Over the years, plan to visit a variety of locations.

- Mountaintop
- Island
- Desert
- Lake
- Prairie
- Farmland
- Waterfall
- River
- Forest
- Ocean
- Cave
- Remote/dark sky area

Local Experts

Catch enthusiasm from people engaged with nature, learn from experts, gain experience beyond the scope of everyday exploring

Connect your students with local nature experts by visiting their organizations or inviting them to speak during your nature study time. Nature centers are staffed with people who know a lot about the area. They may run programs as well. Beekeepers may welcome you to their operations and show you their equipment. An organic farmer may give you a tour and tell you how they prevent weeds and feed plants naturally. Your local Department of Natural Resources may give presentations. Look also for an astronomy club, a wildlife rescue nonprofit, a horse ranch, a rock museum, an animal farm, a wind/water/solar power plant, a family-owned orchard, and a fishing club.

Trail Activities

Trail Activities

Use these activities while you explore a new trail or create new experiences on one you have often traveled.

All the Trails

Discover new places, read maps, analyze and rate trails

Print out the map of a local trail system and commit to hiking every single one. Each week, explore a new trail, using the map to navigate. Use a highlighter to mark where you traveled. By correlating the map with the physical place, students learn spatial reasoning, directionality, and see how symbols are used to communicate information.

After exploring, give the trail a rating of 1, 2, or 3 stars next to the trail name.

> 1 Star= "This trail is ok."
> 2 Stars= "We enjoyed this trail."
> 3 Stars= "We have to come back again!"

Map It

Practice mapping, discover a bird's-eye view of a place

Create a "blob" map of a favorite trail: a very loose, not to scale, imperfect, but understandable depiction. Start by marking the parking lot and trail entrance. Draw a compass rose in the corner. Title the map with the trail or park name. As you walk, sketch the curves and turns of the path and label interesting sights. If your trail needs it, a legend may help. Choose symbols and label them as you need them. Each child and parent could make their own map and compare them to each other at the end. If the trail has a published map, compare your versions to the official one.

You could keep this self-made map in your nature journal or a specific "journal of places," a collection of nature locations explored.

Nature Show and Tell

Encourage an interest in nature, practice public speaking

As you explore an area, have each person collect one thing during the hike. They may change as they go, but in the end, they must settle on just one thing. Each person then does "show and tell" about their find. They should tell as much as they can about the item.

- What is it?

- Why did you choose it?

- Where was it found? How do you think it got there?

Hear/Smell/Touch

Experience nature with your ears, nose, and fingers, communicate using words

We easily observe with our eyes, navigating our steps and thinking about the things we see along the way. For this walk, pay attention to the nature around you using your other senses, noticing what you hear, smell, and feel.

Before setting out, divide your nature journal page into three columns and label them with "I Hear...," "I Smell...," and "I Feel...". As you hike, stop often to listen, smell, and touch the things around you, recording them on your page. As an added challenge, use poetic language to communicate as beautifully and creatively as you can.

- Hear- Describe the bird calls, insect chirps, and wind flitting through the leaves. How would you write each sound as if it were a new word?

- Smell- Take a deep breath through your nose and try to identify the scents in the air. What does this spot smell like? Where is it coming from? Do the smells change along the trail?

- Feel- Touch the things around you. Close your eyes. Write the object name and the textures you feel: smooth, rough, silky, sticky, sharp, wet, dry, hairy, soft, grooved, pitted, etc.

Collection

Engage kids while hiking, accumulate nature study objects to study when hiking is not possible

As you hike, collect interesting things along the way to add to a nature basket or shelf at home. Seed pods, shells, rocks, and bark can be displayed 'as is'. Wildflowers and leaves are best preserved by pressing them in a flower press or sandwiched in printer paper between the pages of a thick book. Dead insects can be saved in small sealed glass jars.

Be sure to read the rules of the trail first. They may prohibit picking flowers or saving leaves. Additionally, it is illegal to possess feathers from some birds, while perfectly fine to keep feathers from others.

Keep your nature collection in your schoolroom or in a basket on your porch. If you are worried about hidden bugs in your treasures, choose an outdoor spot.

These finds are souvenirs from your outdoor experiences that your children will treasure. When inclement weather makes a nature walk impossible, let kids pick something from your collection to study and nature journal.

Rainbow Search

Become aware of the variety of colors and shades in nature

As you hike, work together to collect one thing from each color of the rainbow: red, orange, yellow, green, blue, indigo, violet. This simple search can be done with a wide range of ages. Illustrate your findings in ROYGBIV order in your nature journal.

- Which colors were the easiest to find? Which were the hardest? Why?

Run Ahead

Build observation, memory, and communication skills

Let your children run a safe distance ahead and find something that interests them. Tell them to remember as much as they can about it and return when they are ready to describe it to you in detail. Listen carefully and then ask questions to test their observation skills. About how big was it compared to you? What did it feel like? Where was it found? Was it by itself with others like it? When they have exhausted their knowledge, go with them to see it yourself. (This activity is based on Charlotte Mason's "Sight-Seeing," described in "Home Education" on pages 46-47.)

Trail Guide

Get to know an area well, work on a project, develop leadership skills, practice public speaking

Prepare to be trail guides to lead a hike for grandparents or friends. Visit the trail on your own first, making notes in your nature journal of the things to point out- birds that frequent the area, trees that grow here, and anything that should not be missed. Rate the difficulty of hiking the trail (easy, medium, hard) and decide what the travelers should wear and bring, such as waterproof boots, binoculars, or bug spray. Invite your guests and let the kids take the lead, sharing their knowledge and excitement.

Clean Up Crew

Improve a nature area, learn about trail upkeep, appreciate the trails

Volunteer through the local parks department, community garden, or nature organization to clear invasive species and maintain a nature area. They will give you the training you need and possibly also provide the tools. This type of work is a much-needed service and it is a way to give back to the organizations that preserve the natural areas you love to explore.

TRAIL ACTIVITIES

Worship in the Woods

Make the connection between Creator and creation

Sing about the beauty of creation while in the midst of it. Select songs like "For the Beauty of the Earth," "All Creatures of Our God and King," "Joyful, Joyful We Adore Thee," and "All Things Bright and Beautiful." Sing a cappella or play a portable instrument.

Night Hike

Explore a nature area after dark, compare a habitat between day and night

Walk a familiar trail at night, if open. Bring a flashlight and travel quietly. Stop and listen for sounds. Shine your light up in tree branches to see if you can spot nocturnal animals like owls or raccoons. When back in the car, compare this to your usual daytime explorations.

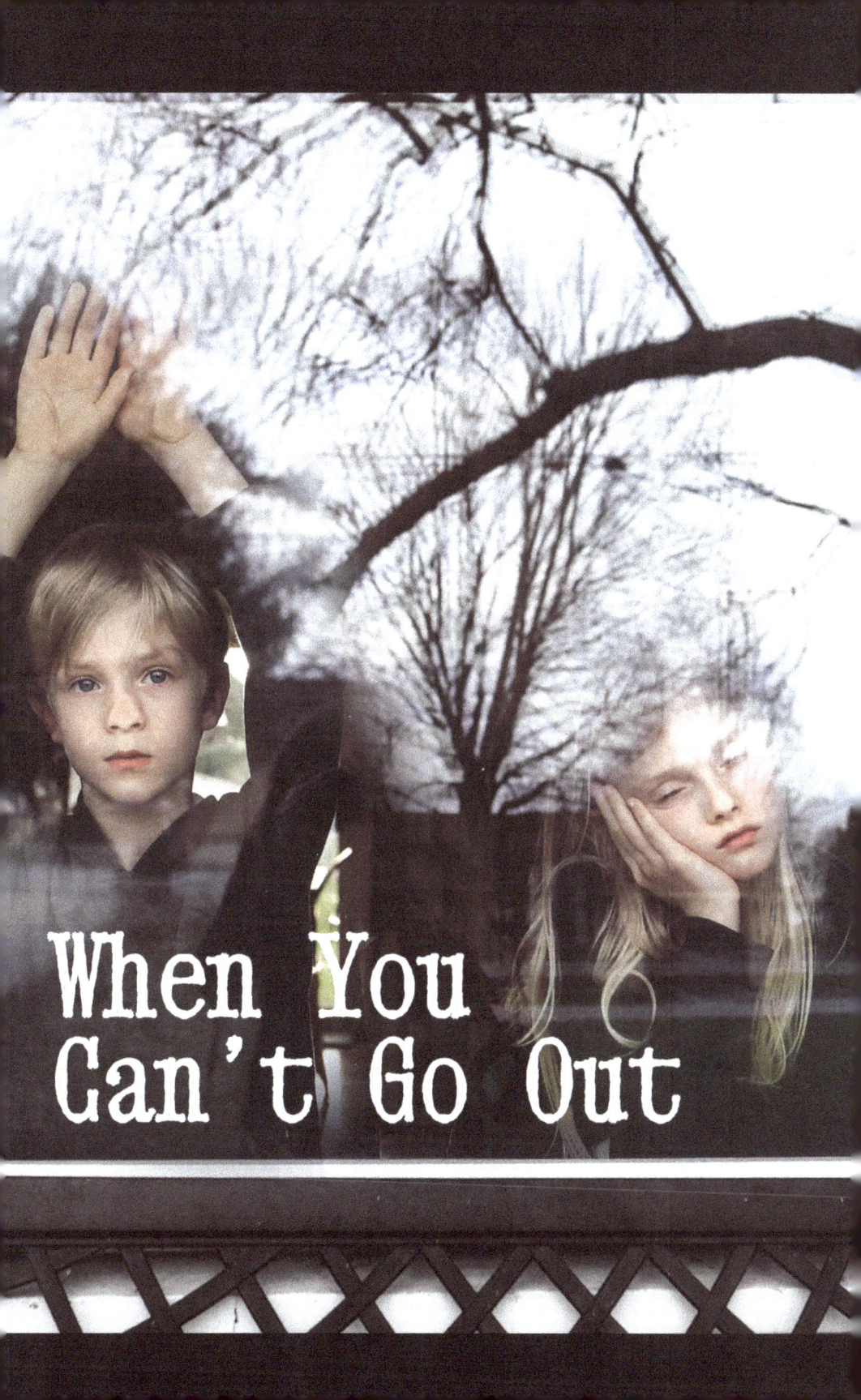

When You
Can't Go Out

When You Can't Go Out...

Days with storms raging, seasons with babies tagging along, or times of illness may call for reliance on more indirect sources of nature experiences. Thankfully we are blessed with an abundance of options as close as the internet and the local library.

Videos

On days when nature study is on the schedule, but you cannot head outside, pull up videos on the topic you are studying. Search "ant colony," "polar animals," or "tornados." It is surprising how many videos have been made in this age of information.

While children will learn more when they discover nature in the wild, there are times and uses for videos. They may give the child exposure to something not native to their area. Videos can show them nature they cannot observe on their own like photosynthesis and the process of rock formation. Children are put in touch with people who are excited and knowledgeable about the topic.

After watching the video, ask them to tell you what it was about in their own words. Ask them what they are wondering about. This may lead to more searching to answer those questions. In their nature journals, have them draw and write about what they learned.

Field Guide Study

Another option for inside days is to have the children flip through a field guide and pick something specific to study. A good guide includes a photograph and information. In their nature journals, the children can draw from the photograph and write about what they read.

Nature Books

Reading a book on a single nature study topic can give an overall view to the child. Books on animal classification, for example, help the child to systematize the knowledge they have gained for themselves about animals they have already encountered.

Like videos, another use for nature books is learning about science topics that cannot be easily observed. A book on the human body teaches the child what is inside their skin. A book about microorganisms opens up a world that is too tiny to see with their eyes. A book about the jungle ecosystem gives them an experience with a habitat that they would not have otherwise.

Use these supporting resources when needed, but keep heading outside for a firsthand nature study!

AUTHOR

Acknowledgements

I am heavily indebted to the work of Charlotte Mason, Anna Botsford Comstock, and John Muir Laws. From them I came to love nature and learned how to study it.

A special thank you is due to those who dedicated their time to help clarify my ideas, catch typos, and correct grammar: Jen Tarmann, Becky Wilkinson, Marilyn Current, Aleshia Cramblet, and several other friends who shared valuable feedback. This project is so much better because of you.

Finally, this book would not have been but for the many nature outings with my children and their friends. These experiences inspired the lesson ideas and allowed me to take them from the page to real life. Thank you, Olivia, Calvin, Korban, Olivia Grace, Josey, Harrison, Lincoln, Hadassah, Eitan, Abigail, Abraham, Eliana, Issac, Braysen, Bria, Britton, Zaya, Noble, Isley, Abri, Elana, Levi, Lillian, Griffin, Truman, Sumner, Elias, Josiah, Charlotte, Elliot, Ella, Beckett, Ashton, Hannah, Rachel, Mearah, Lucas, Arabella, Everly, Sarai, Addyson, and Lily. I love learning with you!

Author

Jamie Current is a homeschooling mom of three, pastor's wife, photographer, and lover of all things in God's creation. She developed this book from the wealth of ideas generated while leading groups of kids into nature every week.

Together with her family, she has lived near the breezy shores of Lake Michigan, the bustle of downtown Chicago, the peaceful rice paddies of South Korea, and now resides in the vast prairie fields of America's heartland. The photographs in this book are of her own kids taken while on nature study outings.

She may be reached via email at Naturestudycollective@gmail.com.

www.ingramcontent.com/pod-product-compliance
Lightning Source LLC
Chambersburg PA
CBHW052011030426
42334CB00029BA/3173